WRITER'S COMPANION

Marcella Frank
American Language Institute, New York University

PRENTICE-HALL, INC., ENGLEWOOD CLIFFS, NEW JERSEY 07632

Library of Congress Cataloging in Publication Data

FRANK, MARCELLA.
    Writer's companion.

    Includes index.
    1. English language—Text-books for foreigners.
2. English language—Rhetoric. 3. English language
—Usage. I. Title.
PE1128.F67 1983   808′.042   82-15154
ISBN 0-13-969790-X

© 1983 by Prentice-Hall, Inc., Englewood Cliffs, N.J. 07632

All rights reserved. No part of this book
may be reproduced in any form or
by any means without permission in writing
from the publisher.

Printed in the United States of America

10 9 8 7 6 5 4

Editorial/production supervision and design by Virginia Rubens
Cover design by Ray Lundgren
Manufacturing buyer: Harry P. Baisley

0-13-969790-X

PRENTICE-HALL INTERNATIONAL, INC., *London*
PRENTICE-HALL OF AUSTRALIA PTY. LIMITED, *Sydney*
PRENTICE-HALL DO BRAZIL, LTDA., *Rio de Janeiro*
PRENTICE-HALL CANADA INC., *Toronto*
PRENTICE-HALL OF INDIA PRIVATE LIMITED, *New Delhi*
PRENTICE-HALL OF JAPAN, INC., *Tokyo*
PRENTICE-HALL OF SOUTHEAST ASIA PTE. LTD., *Singapore*
WHITEHALL BOOKS LIMITED, *Wellington, New Zealand*

Contents

Preface *v*
To the Teacher *vii*
To the Student: Rhetorical Principles of Writing *x*

Index of Usage and Rhetoric *1*
Grammar Review and Practice *93*
    UNIT ONE: Understanding Sentences *94*
    UNIT TWO: Parts of Speech *100*
    UNIT THREE: Complex Structures *110*

Answers to Grammar Exercises *131*
Symbol Chart for Correction of Compositions *137*
Index *141*

Preface

Writer's Companion is intended as a composition aid for high intermediate and advanced students of English as a second or a foreign language. It can also be useful to students in remedial English classes.

While designed to accompany the author's *Writing from Experience,* *Writer's Companion* can also be used with any other composition text or it can be the sole text in a composition class.

Writer's Companion has a unique purpose. It is not a handbook or a reference book as such, but *a compact guide to help students avoid errors as they write and especially as they correct errors after they have written their compositions.* The main part of the text, the Index of Usage and Rhetoric, is keyed to the items in a chart of correction symbols, which is an integral part of this text. Since both the correction chart and the Index are in alphabetical order, students can easily find the information they are looking for.

The entries are on both the sentence and the paragraph levels. The greater part of the entries deal with problems of sentence construction. Some of these items are for narrower corrective purposes—for example, those on dangling constructions, fragments, and subject–verb agreement. Other items are concerned with broader areas of usage where errors are likely to be made—for example, the items on verbs, punctuation, and spelling.

The entries on the paragraph level are essentially for those students who are advanced enough to make corrections for paragraphing. They involve the basic rhetorical principles of paragraph construction and are presented in relation to their function in the entire composition. They include paragraph development in general, introductions, conclusions, transitions between paragraphs, and connections within paragraphs.

The chart of correction symbols enables the teacher to indicate to the

PREFACE

student the kind of fault that needs to be corrected. Because the chart contains brief explanations for each fault, it can also serve as a checklist for students.

The self-help aspect of the Index and the chart of correction symbols should be apparent to both teacher and student. Students are provided with a system for making their own corrections as directed by the correction symbols. Students can also strengthen individual areas of weakness by being assigned specific items in the Index.

While *Writer's Companion* does not claim to be a handbook on writing, the text does contain an introductory note to the student giving a brief summary of the rhetorical principles of writing, such as unity, continuity, proportion. Like the entries in the Index dealing with paragraph construction, this note on rhetoric is for the benefit of the more advanced students.

The text also includes a brief grammar review section with exercises for those students whose background in English structure is inadequate to get the full advantage of the explanations in the Index. For example, students cannot really correct such errors as fragments and run-on sentences unless they know what the parts of a sentence are. This section gives a quick overview of sentences, parts of speech, and complex structures. Depending on the needs of the students, this Grammar Review and Practice section can be used in whole or in part for class work. Also, the answers that are given in the text enable students to do much of the practice work on their own, thus providing still another opportunity for self-help.

The author feels that the materials in this text—the Index and correction chart, and the Grammar Review and Practice section—offer in one text all the supplementary materials that are needed in a composition class to take care of students' individual needs. They thus permit the teacher to concentrate on the task of composition writing itself without having to spend large amounts of class time explaining matters of usage at the sentence level.

To the Teacher

Correcting compositions can be a very frustrating experience for the teacher. Many of us have found that, after we have spent long hours carefully correcting compositions, students have barely glanced at the corrections, or they have mechanically incorporated the corrections in their rewritten compositions. What ought to have been the final step in the active process of writing a composition has thus been merely an empty exercise resulting in little learning.

The materials in this text provide a mechanism that enables students to learn actively by making their own corrections. The chart of correction symbols gives the teacher a simple means of labeling mistakes for student correction. The Index of Usage and Rhetoric, since it covers only the items on the chart, gives students easy access to the information they need to make corrections. With these two resources available to students, the teacher is able to save time in correcting papers, and students can participate actively in the final step in composition writing, thereby increasing the possibility that the learning will be retained.

The items that have been chosen for correction are based on the author's many years of experience in teaching composition. Abundant samples of student errors have been drawn upon to determine not only which errors should be labeled by symbols, but how much explanation needs to be given in the Index. However, in order to keep the Index as clear and concise as possible, some details that both the teacher and the student might be looking for have been omitted. The author's *Modern English: A Practical Reference Guide* can be consulted for additional reference information.

The teacher will find that many of the items on the correction chart are similar to those found in Freshman English handbooks. However, a

TO THE TEACHER

number of omissions and changes have been made in order to keep the list short and manageable and also to meet the needs of students of English as a second or a foreign language. Among the faults omitted are those that really need to be corrected by the teacher, such as awkward or unidiomatic usage, as well as those that are concerned with finer points of style, reasoning, and diction. Among the changes made are the combination of several faults under one symbol. For example, under the symbol **pro** (pronoun) are included not only the form of pronouns, but pronoun reference, pronoun shift, and pronoun number, all of which have separate symbols in Freshman English handbooks. Under **P** (punctuation) are included all problems in punctuation, including run-on sentences.[1]

Because some of the correction symbols are so comprehensive, the teacher might find it desirable, at least at the beginning, to include a sub-symbol—for example, **pro (ref)**, **V (tense)**, or **P (run-on)**. Also, later on in the term, some of the symbols can be shortened—for example, **Agr** for agreement, **F** for fragment—since students not only will be more familiar with the error but will be able to check it easily because of the alphabetical listing in the correction chart and the Index. Eventually, after students become even more familiar with the type of errors represented by the symbols, each error might be merely underlined.

Some symbols whose meanings are obvious have been omitted from the correction chart because they do not need entries in the Index. The teacher may want to include the following:

∧	omission of a word or words
?	illegible, or I don't understand this
/	separate the words

In classes with more advanced students, teachers might also wish to use their own symbols for some of the faults given below.

Faults in Reasoning

1. Overgeneralization, of the "all or none" variety.
2. The use of insufficient or invalid evidence.
3. The use of irrelevant, unnecessary, or unclear details or arguments.
4. The omission of a step in the reasoning, or an unfinished idea.
5. The use of a judgment stated as a fact.

---

[1] In this text the term *run-on* includes both the kind of fault in which two sentences are joined together unacceptably with a comma (also called *comma fault* or *comma splice*) and the kind with no punctuation at all (also called *run-together* or *fused* sentence).

Faults in Diction

1. Trite expression.
2. Shift in tone.
3. Mixed metaphor.

Although careful thought was given to the selection and coverage of each symbol on the correction chart, it is inevitable that there will be some omissions and some overlapping. Also, some usages might with equal justification have been put under another symbol. There will be no real problem if the teacher uses some symbols that are different from the ones in the correction chart. However, the teacher should keep in mind that the Index gives information about a particular usage under the symbol in the chart. This is especially important if items from the Index are being assigned for study by individual students.

If the teacher feels that students are not yet ready to handle the number of correction symbols on the correction chart, it would be advisable to begin with the starred symbols, which cover more elementary types of errors, and then gradually introduce the other symbols.

To encourage students to help themselves still further in overcoming their mistakes, the teacher might suggest that they keep a list of corrections, with the surrounding context if necessary, and that they review this list from time to time.

For those classes that need additional practice with grammatical usages, the teacher might have students work with one or both parts of the author's *Modern English: Exercises for Non-native Speakers*.

To the Student: Rhetorical Principles of Writing

Much of the Index of Usage and Rhetoric that follows contains information about such matters as grammar, punctuation, and spelling that can help you as you write sentences. The Index also gives information that can guide you in writing paragraphs. However, to be a successful writer, you also need to understand and apply the important rhetorical principles that concern the organization and the development of compositions. Such principles, although not always followed strictly in all kinds of writing, are very important for the type of writing that is required in academic work.

These rhetorical principles are summarized here, along with suggestions for applying them.

1. *The composition must have unity.*

A composition must be unified by one central idea. It is not enough to write about a subject in general. You must be able to make a definite point about the subject. This point is your central idea that will control everything you say in the composition.

In order to determine what the central idea of a composition will be, you might start by using one of the following procedures.

A. List your ideas about the general subject of the composition in the random order in which they occur to you.

B. Write a first draft on the general topic without any preliminary plan.

TO THE STUDENT

With either preliminary procedure, the next step is the important one. Try to state in one sentence what seems to be the general direction of your thinking on the subject. In this sentence, which is your "thesis" sentence, the subject of the sentence contains the general topic you are writing about; the predicate contains what you say about this topic.

You may find that your thesis sentence will require you either to write a very long paper or to treat your subject superficially. In this case, narrow down the scope of the sentence to the point where you can develop your supporting points adequately in the assigned length of the composition.

Once you have your central idea expressed in the thesis sentence, you are ready to prepare the working outline that will guide you in writing the final draft of your composition. The following procedures are useful in setting up the outline based on your central idea.

A. Eliminate the points from your preliminary outline or draft that do not contribute to the central idea. Add others that might strengthen the central idea.

B. Organize smaller points as subpoints under larger points, making sure that none of the points overlap. At this stage you may need to add some larger, more general headings under which you can put several of your smaller points.

C. Check to see that your main points are of equal importance and at the same level of generalization.

D. Arrange the main points and their subpoints in the most effective order. Common types of order are by time or space, by logical relationships, or by a progression from less important to more important.

To make clear what your main points and their subpoints are, use the standard form of outlining.

I. (Roman numerals for main points)
    A. (Capital letters for subdivision of main points)
        1. (Further subdivision)
            a. (Still further subdivision)

For example, if you were making a comparison between your language and English, you might have an outline like the following:

TO THE STUDENT

A Comparison Between My Language and English

I. Writing system
   A. Characters used
      1. My language
      2. English
   B. Punctuation
      1. My language
      2. English

II. Grammatical system
   A. Word order
      1. My language
      2. English
   B. Word endings
      1. My language
      2. English

All the items on the outline can be written either as phrases (as in the outline above) or as full sentences, but the same form should be followed throughout. Also, there should be at least two items under each subdivision (a single item can be included with the main heading).

2. *The composition must have a beginning, a middle (a body), and an end.*
The composition should have an introduction that is interesting enough to catch the reader's attention. The introduction usually treats the subject in general terms and often suggests how the subject will be treated in the composition.

The body is the main part of the composition. It contains the development of the points on the outline. The opening sentence of each paragraph refers to one of these points and the balance of the paragraph gives supporting details for this point. The usual pattern of development in the body, therefore, is a succession of general-to-particular paragraphs.

The conclusion rounds out the composition by opening up from the specific content of the composition to the more general subject again, to leave the reader with a final thought about the central idea of the composition.

Thus the composition begins and ends with statements that are more general than the main points in the body of the composition.

(More information about beginnings and ends of compositions can be found in the Index entries under **Introduction** and **Conclusion**.)

3. *The composition must have continuity.*

All the parts of the composition must be connected in such a way that the reader can see their relationships.

A. There must be a transition that connects the general statements of the introduction with the narrower content that forms the body of the composition.

B. There must be transitional connections between all paragraphs. The opening sentence of a paragraph plays an important role in such connections. This sentence is a bridge between two points: the point of the preceding paragraph and the point of the new paragraph it introduces.

C. There must be connections, expressed or understood, between the details in each paragraph so that their role in the development of the main idea of the paragraph is clear.

(More information about continuity may be found in the Index entries under **Transition** [connection between paragraphs] and **Connection** [connection within paragraphs].)

4. *The composition must be guided by a sense of proportion.*

An introduction or a conclusion should be in proportion to the length of the main part of the composition. Also, more space should be devoted to more important ideas than to less important ones.

5. *The composition must have well-constructed paragraphs.*

Each new point from the outline should be in a separate paragraph. The opening sentence of a paragraph should give some indication of the subject that is to be developed in the paragraph, and the rest of the paragraph should be limited to this one subject.

The paragraph should be developed sufficiently so that the reader can feel that the point has been convincingly supported. Also, all the supporting details should be clearly connected.

(The Index gives more information about paragraphing under **Paragraphs.**)

Index of Usage and Rhetoric

Items in this Index are keyed to the symbols on the correction chart.

agree	Agreement (between subject and verb)	p. 3
ap	Apostrophe	4
art	Article	5
C	Capital letter	8
⌒	Close up	9
comp	Comparison	10
concl	Conclusion	12
con	Connection (within paragraphs)	13
coor	Coordination (especially overcoordination)	15
dangl	Dangling	16
frag	Fragment	17
H	Hyphen	18
inform	Informal	21
intro	Introduction	21
neg	Negative	22
N	Number (of nouns and adjectives)	23
par	Paragraph development	25
¶	New paragraph	
no	No new paragraph	
//	Parallelism	27
prep	Preposition	29
pro	Pronoun	32
P	Punctuation	36
	Commas in sentences with introductory or final grammatical elements	37

INDEX OF USAGE AND RHETORIC

	Commas in sentences with interrupting elements	38
	Commas and semicolons in combined independent sentences	39
	Commas in a series (with *and, or*)	39
	Commas and quotation marks in direct speech	40
	Other uses of punctuation for sentence structure (colon, semicolon, dash)	40
	Unacceptable commas (including run-on sentences)	41
	Unacceptable semicolons	43
repet	Repetitious	44
SS	Sentence structure	45
	Summary of sentence structures	46
sp	Spelling	49
	Spelling rules for *ie* and *ei* words	50
	Spelling rules for adding final elements	50
	Spelling changes in prefixes before certain letters	51
	Word pairs often confused because of similarities in sound	53
	160 frequently misspelled words	55
trans	Transition (between paragraphs)	57
vague	Vague	59
V	Verb	60
	Tense forms	61
	Special notes on verb forms	64
	Uses of the tenses	67
	Special uses of the tense forms	70
	Agreement of the verb and the subject	73
	Verbals (infinitives with *to,* participles with *-ing* or *-ed*)	73
	Modal auxiliaries	76
	Irregular verbs	79
WF	Word form	82
WO	Word order	84
∿	Reverse the word order	
wordy	Wordy	89
WW	Wrong word	90

INDEX OF USAGE AND RHETORIC

agree

agreement   (between subject and verb)

1. The verb must agree in number (singular or plural) with its subject.

>The *girl sings* well. (a singular verb with a singular subject)
>The *girls sing* well. (a plural verb with a plural subject)

If auxiliaries are used with the verb, only the *first* auxiliary agrees with the subject.

>Her *husband has* been working in the same company for a long time.

(See **Verb, 5,** for more information on subject-auxiliary agreement.)

2. If the subject is long, the verb agrees with the *main word* of the subject. (This main word occurs *before* a prepositional phrase or any other postmodifier.)

>The *architecture* of these buildings *is* very interesting.

However, if the main word in the subject expresses a *part* (*some, all, half,* etc.), the verb agrees with the noun in a following *of* phrase.

>Most of the *cake was* eaten.
>Most of the *cookies were* eaten.

3. If the word *one* is used before *of,* the verb is singular.

>*One* of the tallest buildings in New York City *is* the Empire State Building. (Note that the noun in the *of* phrase—*buildings*—is plural.)

4. If *each* or *every* is used with the subject, the verb must be *singular,* even though the meaning may be plural.

>*Each* student *has* to fill out a special form.
>*Everybody is* leaving early today.

5. Two (or more) subjects joined by *and* require a plural verb.

>Fruit *and* vegetables *are* good for the health.

6. If two parts of the subject are joined by *or* or *nor,* the verb agrees with the second part.

>Either Mr. Johnson or his *sons are* guilty.

7. The verb in an adjective clause must agree with the word it refers to.

>Those *people* who *come* to the stadium early are going to get special prizes.

8. A noncountable subject requires a singular verb.

>The *information* in these reports *is* not accurate.

3

INDEX OF USAGE AND RHETORIC

9. A subject whose main word is an *-ing* or a *to* form requires a singular verb.

> *Playing* with matches *is* a dangerous pastime.
> *To make* mistakes *is* only human.

10. A collective noun referring to a group (*family, committee, jury,* for example) usually takes a singular verb in American English.

> The *committee is* meeting now.

However, if the speaker is thinking of the individual members of the group, a plural verb is used.

> The *committee have* disagreed among themselves.

11. In a sentence containing a form of *be* that joins two nouns, the rule is that the verb agrees with the subject.

> To me, *happiness is* two things.

However, it is best to revise such a sentence.

> To me, *happiness consists* of two things.

12. *The number of* requires a singular verb; *a number of* requires a plural verb.

> *The number of* students who pass this test *is* small.
> *A number of* students always fail this test. (*a number = some* or *many*)

ap

apostrophe

1. Most apostrophes mark either the contraction of verbs with other words, or the possessive forms of nouns.

A. *Contractions with verbs (informal usage)*

    (1) Contraction of auxiliaries (or the independent verbs *have* and *be*) with *not*.

> are + not = aren't (the apostrophe replaces the omitted *o* from *not*). Exceptions are can't, won't.

    (2) Contraction of tense auxiliaries with *the subject.*

        a. With a *pronoun* subject:

> it is = it's (do not confuse this contraction with *its*, the possessive of *it*)
> who is = who's (do not confuse this contraction with *whose*, the possessive of *who*)

b. With a *noun* subject:

The *train's* just arrived. ('s = *has*)
The *train's* here. ('s = *is*)

B. *Possessive of nouns (usually for living beings)*

's with a singular noun:

the *girl's* mother

's with a plural noun that does not end in -*s:*

the *women's* clubs, the *people's* choice

's with a plural noun:

the *girls'* mothers

An *'s* may also be used with nouns other than those that refer to living beings.

time: *a month's delay*
natural phenomena: *the sun's rays*
political entities: *France's economy*
groups of people working together: *the committee's decision*

2. No apostrophe is used for possessive forms of personal pronouns.

A country must protect *its* citizens.
This book is *yours* (*hers, his, ours, theirs*).

However, the possessive of the impersonal pronoun *one* requires an apostrophe.

One should always try to do *one's* best.

3. In phrases that are derived from full sentences, an *'s* (or *s'*) ending is used with nouns that were originally subjects.

Sentence	Phrase
Mr. Black retired early.	Mr. Black's early retirement
The Pilgrims landed at Plymouth Rock.	The Pilgrims' landing at Plymouth Rock.

art

article

The definite article *the* generally signals a *particular* person or thing that has been singled out from others.

the student sitting next to you

INDEX OF USAGE AND RHETORIC

The indefinite article *a* signals an *unspecified one* among others.

>*a* student sitting in the front row

The following rules are among the most important in the use of articles.

1. An article (or another determiner) *must* appear with a singular countable noun.

>*The* letter was sent yesterday.
>
>*A* (or *the*) lion is a wild animal. (*Lion* is a class word in this general statement. The plural *lions* [with no *the*] may also be used to express this same generalization.)

2. *A* is not generally used with noncountable nouns.[1] If indefinite reference is desired with such nouns, *some* is used instead.

>I need some milk.
>
>Please give me some information.

3. *The* usually does not occur with noncountable nouns in general statements.

>Everyone requires food, water, and shelter.

4. However, *the* is used with *both countable and noncountable nouns* in the following instances:

>**A.** A modifier follows the noun (especially if the sentence refers to a particular situation).
>
>| | |
>|---|---|
>| COUNTABLE NOUN | *The* eggs *in the refrigerator* are still good. |
>| NONCOUNTABLE NOUN | *The* milk *in the refrigerator* is still good. |

However, if the noun is considered unknown, or if it represents one out of others, *a* is used with a singular countable noun.

>*A* man *in the audience* suddenly started to shout.

>**B.** The noun refers to an object in the environment that is familiar to or near the speaker.
>
>| | |
>|---|---|
>| COUNTABLE NOUN | Let's go to *the* park near *the* river. |
>| NONCOUNTABLE NOUN | Put *the* milk and *the* butter in the refrigerator. |

---

[1] See **Number, 1B,** for a list of types of noncountable nouns.

INDEX OF USAGE AND RHETORIC

5. In extended speech, the first time a person or object is mentioned, *a* is used. Further references to the person or thing are with *the*.

I recently got *a* new job. *The* job is hard but interesting.

6. *The* usually precedes superlatives (***the*** *prettiest,* ***the*** *most beautiful*) and ordinals (***the*** *first,* ***the*** *second*).

7. *A* is required after *such* or *what* used with a singular countable noun.

She is such *a* pretty girl.
What *a* pretty girl she is.

8. For geographic names, *the* is used if:

A. The name includes a word for a political union.

the British *Commonwealth,* the Venezuelan *Republic,* the Soviet *Union*

B. The name includes an *of* phrase.

the Gulf *of Mexico,* the City *of New York*

C. The name is plural.

the Rocky *Mountains,* the *Philippines*

D. The word refers to a body of water other than a lake or a bay.

the Nile *River,* the Mediterranean *Sea*

9. Some words may be used either in a noncountable sense as an abstract idea (a concept) or in a countable sense as something that has actual existence.

NONCOUNTABLE SENSE	The child learns through *imitation*. (*Imitation* is a concept.)
COUNTABLE SENSE	This picture is a good *imitation*. (*Imitation* is a concrete object.)

10. *A* may be used with some noncountable nouns to mean *a kind of.*

We live in *a* (= a kind of) *society* that is becoming more permissive.

Compare with:

The (= the particular one) *society* that we live in is becoming more permissive.

and

Society (a concept) is becoming more permissive.

7

INDEX OF USAGE AND RHETORIC

11. *The* is required before adjectives used alone as nouns.

> *The* French celebrate Bastille Day on July 14.
> *The* rich get richer while *the* poor get poorer.

(Note that the verb is plural to agree with the "understood" noun *people*.)

12. *The* may be used in a sentence with two parts, each part beginning with *the* + a comparative.

> *The longer* he worked, *the easier* his job became.
> *The more* he learned about life, *the more cynical* he became.

13. *The* is used in *of* phrases after expressions of quantity.

> Most ⎫
> All ⎪ of *the* students (in this class) passed the examination.
> Many ⎬
> Ten ⎭

C

capital letter

The following types of words should begin with capital letters.

1. The first word in a sentence.

> This is a composition book.

2. Days of the week and months of the year.

> Saturday, Wednesday; January, March

3. Words referring to nationality, whether the words are adjectives or nouns.

ADJECTIVES	a French teacher
	a Spanish custom
NOUNS	He is a Frenchman.
	She is a Spaniard.

4. Words referring to religion, whether the words are adjectives or nouns.

ADJECTIVES	a Catholic church
	a Buddhist priest
NOUNS	She is a good Catholic.
	He is a Buddhist.

Holy works are also capitalized.

> the Bible, the Koran

INDEX OF USAGE AND RHETORIC

5. Names of holidays, including the word *Day* or *Eve*.

   New Year's Day, Christmas Eve

6. Geographical names.

   the Mississippi River, the Rocky Mountains
   (Note that words like *River* and *Mountains* are also capitalized.)

7. Points of the compass naming a specific geographic area which is considered as a unit.

   the East, the Middle West (of the United States), Central America, Southeast Asia (but northern Europe)

No capital is used when the point merely indicates a direction.

   to the north of Mexico, travel south

8. Government agencies or bodies.

   the Armed Forces, the Navy

9. Historical periods, events, and documents.

   the Industrial Revolution, the Renaissance, the Bill of Rights, the Middle Ages

10. Political parties.

    the Democratic party, the Labor party (Sometimes the word *party* is capitalized.)

11. Names of streets and avenues.

    Fifth Avenue, Houston Street (Note that Avenue and Street are capitalized.)

12. The salutation in a letter, and the first word of the closing of the letter.

SALUTATION	Gentlemen:	Dear Mrs. Jones:
CLOSING	Yours truly,	Sincerely yours,

13. Buildings and public places or structures.

    the White House, the Statue of Liberty, the Empire State Building

14. In titles of books, stories, plays, poems, the first and last words and all other words except articles and short prepositions or conjunctions.

    A Farewell to Arms, *The Merchant of Venice*

close up

This symbol indicates that two parts of a word should be written together with no break between the parts.

INDEX OF USAGE AND RHETORIC

Words whose parts are sometimes incorrectly separated are: *some⌢times, house⌢work, an⌢other, may⌢be, now⌢a⌢days, in⌢as⌢much.* *Cannot* is usually written as one word in American English.

1. Prefixes like *over-, under-, extra-, anti-, non-, semi-, counter-* are now usually joined directly to the rest of the word.

> **underweight, extrasensory, counterrevolutionary, nonconformist, antisocial, semicolon**

2. Suffixes like *-self, -like, -wide* are also joined to the rest of the word.

> **herself, childlike, worldwide**

3. Combinations with *-one, -body, -thing, -where* are written together without a break.

> **someone, anybody, everything, nowhere** (but *no one*)

4. There is a growing tendency in American English for commonly used compound words to be written with no break between the parts.

> **drugstore, bookkeeper,** a **breakdown** (but *to break down*)

Dictionaries may differ in the way they record some of these compounds.

comp

comparison

In making comparisons, the correct usage should be observed.

1. *Forms for comparison of adjectives*

	Comparing Two Units (Comparative)	Comparing Three or More Units (Superlative)
one-syllable adjectives	_____-er than (tall*er than*)	the _____-est (*the* tall*est*)
adjectives of three or more syllables	**more** _____ **than** (*more* beautiful *than*)	**the most** _____ (*the most* beautiful)
two-syllable adjectives except those ending in:	**more** _____ **than** (*more* useful *than*)	**the most** _____ (*the most* useful)
-y	_____-er than (dirti*er than*)	the _____-est (*the* dirti*est*)
-le	_____-er than (simpl*er than*)	the _____-est (*the* simpl*est*)

Some two-syllable adjectives may be compared either way:

narrower *or* more narrow
cleverer *or* more clever
handsomer *or* more handsome

If you are in doubt about which form to use for comparison, choose *more, most*. Never use both *more* and the *-er* ending together.

2. *Prepositions and conjunctions in comparison*

harder *than*	Some students work harder than others.
the same *as*	The telephone rates are the same as those of last year.
compared *with*	New York is very dirty compared with many other cities.
in comparison *with*	In comparison with other cities, New York is very dirty.
different *from* (informal: *than*)	His behavior is very different from that of his brother.
similar *to*	Spanish is similar to French in some ways.
as _____ as (also so _____ as after a negative verb)	She doesn't spend as (*or* so) much money as she used to.
a similarity *between*	There is a strong similarity between the two sisters.
a difference *between*	The differences between the two languages are very great.
a comparison *between*	A comparison between the two languages reveals many differences.

3. *Articles in comparison*

The must be used with the word *same* and with superlatives.

the same
the most _____, the _____-est[2]

4. *Omissions in the second part of a comparison*

A. To avoid repeating a word or phrase in the second part of a comparison, substitute the word *that* (for a noncountable word), *the one(s)*, or *those*. This substitution is especially important in formal English.

---

[2] When the word *most* is used informally to mean *very*, *a* may come before *most:* She was a most (= very) devoted mother.

The buildings in this city are taller than *those* (= the buildings) in my city. The word order of Turkish is different from *that* (= the word order) of English.

B. To avoid repeating a predicate in a comparison, substitute an auxiliary for this predicate.

Young children need more milk than older people *do*.
(*do* = need milk)

The second part of the comparison can be further shortened by omitting even the auxiliary.

Young children need more milk than older people.

Sometimes omission of part of the structure in the second part of the comparison causes a problem in meaning.

She gave her grandson more money than her son.

To make the meaning clear, such a sentence can be rewritten as:

She gave her grandson more money than her son did.

or

She gave her grandson more money than she gave her son.

C. If a personal pronoun appears alone as a subject in the second part of a comparison, formal usage requires that this pronoun be in subject form.

My brother is much taller than *I*.

However, in informal English the object form is very common.

My brother is much taller than *me*.

5. Use of other *in the second unit of a comparison*

If one member of a class is being compared with the remaining members of the class, *other* is required in the second unit.

New York City is larger than any *other* city in the United States.

concl

conclusion

In a composition, the reader expects some sort of conclusion that rounds off the discussion of the subject. Since final position is one of emphasis, a reference to the importance of what has been said in the composition often appears in the conclusion.

There are several ways of writing effective conclusions.

1. Summarize the main points of the composition, stating them in some emphatic form.

2. Emphasize the significance of the central idea of the composition.

3. Leave a question in the reader's mind related to the central idea of the composition.

4. Suggest a solution to a problem raised in the composition.

5. Close with an appropriate quotation from poetry or prose.

6. Go back to the special situation or anecdote used in the introduction.

Do not end a composition on an unimportant detail or incorporate within the conclusion a new point that requires further discussion.

A conclusion may not be necessary if the composition brings itself naturally to an end at a certain paragraph (this is especially true for a narrative account) or if it ends with a significant detail.

A conclusion should read as though it is a natural part of the composition and should never be merely "tacked on" because the writer knows that a conclusion is required.

con

connection (within paragaphs)

Since the paragraph represents one whole unit of thought, the need for continuity is even greater within paragraphs than between paragraphs, where the separation in space permits a somewhat looser connection between one paragraph and the next. There should be no missing steps in the development of the main idea of the paragraph; all details that are needed to carry forward the idea should be included. Also, all connections between the details of the paragraph should be clear. Sometimes these connections are obvious merely from the context; one sentence runs smoothly into the next. At other times, however, these connections must be expressed.

There are a number of techniques for establishing connections between the details of a paragraph. Especially important are those that provide coherence by pointing back to what has been mentioned already. The following are some of these techniques.

1. Use personal pronouns or the impersonal *one* to refer back to nouns.

> Walt Whitman is perhaps the greatest American poet of the nineteenth century. *His Leaves of Grass* influenced many poets who came after *him*.
> My country has many holidays. The *one* that I enjoy the most is New Year's Day.

INDEX OF USAGE AND RHETORIC

2. Use "pointing back" pronouns or adverbs that enable the writer to make a connection without your having to repeat part of what has already been said. These pronouns frequently require "summing up" words with them.

> SUCH When I was very young I wanted to be an acrobat. Later I decided to become a violinist. But such ambitions were completely forgotten by the time I entered the university. (Note that *ambitions* is a summing-up word for the two occupations the writer wanted to have.)
>
> THIS, THAT In my country, talking while eating is not considered polite. Today, however, many people disregard *this* rule of etiquette. (Note that *rule of etiquette* is a summing-up word for *talking while eating is not considered polite*.)

If *this* is used alone, care must be taken that what it refers to is perfectly clear. (See **Pronoun, 3,** about the misuse of *this* or *that* to refer too far back to what has already been said.)

> HERE, THERE You must be sure to go to the market place *nearby*.
> (for a place) *There* you will find all kinds of ceramics at reasonable prices.

3. Repeat key expressions, either exactly or in somewhat changed or synonymous form.

> Superstition is an irrational belief that supernatural forces can cause good or bad things to happen. As people are becoming more educated, *superstitious beliefs* are beginning to disappear.

4. Use parallel structure to line up ideas.

> That Edison made many inventions which have changed our way of life is well known. That Edison accomplished so much with only a few hours' sleep a day is not so well known.

5. Move grammatical elements forward in the sentence so that they establish continuity immediately.

> The new teacher opened the classroom door hesitantly. *Awaiting her in the room* was a class of thirty noisy students.

6. Use transitional expressions to indicate certain relationships.

> The young couple were very much in love and talked about getting married. *However,* they knew they would have trouble overcoming their parents' objections.

(See the list of transitional expressions in **Transition** in this Index for various ways of expressing relationships.)

INDEX OF USAGE AND RHETORIC

In addition to the techniques for making connections between the sentences in a paragraph, there are also ways of providing continuity throughout the whole paragraph. This continuity is established in two ways.

1. The logical arrangement of the details. Such an arrangement can be according to time, space, or order of importance. Other types of arrangement are general to particular, particular to general, cause to effect, or effect to cause.

2. The choice of grammatical structures. Retaining the same subject of sentences throughout most of the paragraph makes the movement of thought clear to the writer. The same is true for keeping the same voice—active or passive—as much as possible throughout the paragraph. Shifts in subject or voice interrupt the line of development and slow down the comprehension of the paragraph.

coor

coordination (especially overcoordination)

Coordination refers to the use of grammatical elements of equal rank for ideas considered on the same level of importance.

Coordination can be excessive when too many short, simple sentences or parts of sentences are given equal grammatical rank (coordination). Such sentences have a choppy, monotonous effect, especially if the same word starts some of the sentences. Overcoordination can be avoided by grammatically subordinating some of the ideas to others.

1. *Overcoordination with short, simple sentences*

OVERCOORDINATED:	I was born in 1947.
	More exactly I was born on the third of November, 1947.
	It was in a small town called Petion Ville.
IMPROVED:	I was born on November 3, 1947, in a small town called Petion Ville.
OVERCOORDINATED:	Tokyo is located in the central part of Japan.
	It is the capital.
	It is the biggest and most active city in Japan.
IMPROVED:	Located in the central part of Japan, Tokyo, the capital, is the biggest and most active city in the country.

15

INDEX OF USAGE AND RHETORIC

2. *Overcoordination with* **and:**

OVERCOORDINATED:	I wrote to the University and in one month I was almost ready to come here to study English and social work and also to make new friends, Americans and people from all over the world.
IMPROVED:	One month after I heard from the University, I made my preparations to come here to study English first, then social work. I also hoped to meet new friends, both Americans and people from all over the world.

Often a second clause after *and* can be reduced to a *which, who(m)* or *where* clause, thereby eliminating the *and*.

After the soup, we serve the main course, *and it* (= *which*) usually includes three or four dishes.

Haiti is a mountainous country *and* (= *where*) you can take long walks.

I had many friends, *and most of them* (= *most of whom*) lived in the neighborhood.

dangl
dangling

Many "subject-less" phrases with *-ing* or *-ed* participles depend on the subject of the sentence for their agent. If the subject of the sentence cannot be the agent, the phrase is considered to be "dangling," that is, grammatically unattached. Most dangling phrases occur at the beginning of sentences.

DANGLING:	On *hearing* the sad news, *tears* came to her eyes. (The *tears* are not doing the *hearing*.)
CORRECTION:	On *hearing* the sad news, *she* began to cry.
OR:	When she heard the sad news, tears came to her eyes. (*Heard* now has its own subject.)
DANGLING:	*Damaged* by the storm, *water* began to fill the boat. (The *water* was not *damaged*.)
CORRECTION:	*Damaged* by the storm, *the boat* began to be filled with water.
OR:	Water began to fill the boat after it was damaged by the storm.

Other types of phrases may also dangle if they cannot be clearly attached to a subject.

INDEX OF USAGE AND RHETORIC

DANGLING:	As a child, my parents took me to the beach every summer.
CORRECTION:	As a child, I was taken to the beach every summer.
OR:	When I was a child, my parents took me to the beach every summer.
DANGLING:	To prepare for this test, hard work is required.
CORRECTION:	To prepare for this test, you must work hard.

frag

fragment

A fragment is a part of a sentence that has been improperly cut off from the rest of the sentence with a period. Some acceptable fragments can be found in professional writing, but generally it is best for students to avoid the use of fragments.

Most fragments occur when the final part of a sentence is cut off from the first part. This kind of fault can be corrected in two ways: (1) by using a comma instead of a period, and (2) by changing the fragment to a full sentence.

FRAGMENT:	I would like to study the language first. *Because my English is not very good.*
CORRECTION:	I would like to study the language first, because my English is not very good.
OR:	I would like to study the language first. The reason is that my English is not very good. (Unless the parts of the sentence are long, this is a less likely choice for correction.)

The following are examples of common types of fragments. All these sentences (except the third one below) can be corrected by replacing the period with a comma.

Cutting off a dependent clause:

I believe that women should be treated equally in every respect. *Whether they choose to work or to stay at home.*

Every English word is formed by combining several letters of the alphabet. *While in Chinese, words are formed by combining several characters out of thousands of characters.*

I received my student visa very late. *Which made me nervous because I had to do a lot of things in a hurry.* (In this sentence, if the indefinite *which* is replaced by *this,* a word that is not grammatically dependent on what precedes it, the period may be retained.)

17

Cutting off a phrase:

You should visit these old temples and shrines. *Especially for their beautiful gardens.*

Cutting off a structure with an incomplete verb:

The search party separated. *Some going to the right, some to the left.*
The Greek philosopher Diogenes searched everywhere. *Looking for an honest man.*

Cutting off examples in incomplete sentences:

Whether a mother goes to work will depend on the situation of the individual family. *For example, the desire of the woman, the financial status of the family, and most important, the age of the children.*

Cutting off a listing or enumeration:

The Greek educational system has three levels. *Elementary school, high school, and university.*

Cutting off a phrase beginning with one of the words from the first part of the sentence:

Woman's place is certainly not in the home, because there is a choice. *The choice for a man and a woman to decide together what they want to do with their lives.*

Cutting off a short sentence beginning with *and, or, but, so*:

I graduated from high school in Korea. *So I have a very limited knowledge about the United States.*

H

hyphen

Hyphens are used to connect parts of words and to mark the division of words at the end of a line.

Hyphens within words

There are some differences between American and British usage with respect to hyphens within words. Sometimes even American dictionaries do not agree about the use of hyphens in certain words. There is a growing tendency in the United States to use fewer hyphens.

INDEX OF USAGE AND RHETORIC

The rules given below for the use of hyphens within words are generally followed in the United States.

1. Hyphens in adjective compounds.

   A. Words ending in the *-ing* or *-ed* participle.

   a good-looking girl, a Spanish-speaking student; ready-made clothes, foreign-born workers

   B. A participle plus a preposition used before a noun.

   worn-out shoes[3]
   grown-up behavior

2. Hyphens in noun compounds used in adjective function before nouns.

   a six-year-old child, a ten-foot pole

   Such words are not hyphenated if they are used in the predicate.

   The child is six years old.
   The pole is ten feet high.

3. Hyphens in words with certain prefixes, especially *self-*, *ex-* (meaning former), *all-*, *co-*.

   self-preservation, ex-wife, co-author

4. Hyphens in nouns or adjectives containing phrases within them.

   mother-in-law, wall-to-wall carpet, hit-and-run driver

5. Hyphens in the numbers 21 through 99 when they are written out.

   twenty-one, ninety-nine

6. Hyphens in fractions.

   three-fourths, five-sixths

Hyphens for word division

The hyphen for dividing a word at the end of a line is written in the middle of its space, not at the bottom or at the top.
   Do not use the hyphen to begin a line.

---

[3] When these combinations are used as verbs, they are written as separate words: *wear out, grow up*. Most nouns from such verb–preposition combinations are written as one word: *a handout, a breakdown*.

INDEX OF USAGE AND RHETORIC

Rules for word division

General rule: Divide between syllables of pronunciation

    mul·ti·ply   or·ches·tra

    spe·cial   at·ten·tion (the *ci* and *ti* spelling in these words make one sound /sh/)

Do not divide between the parts of a word that are pronounced as one syllable.

    UNACCEPTABLE: be·cau·se

Specific rules

1. Do not divide words of one syllable of pronunciation.

    UNACCEPTABLE: thro·ugh   gu·ide

When the *-ed* ending is pronounced as /t/ or /d/, it is not a separate syllable of pronunciation. Words like *talked* and *robbed* are one syllable of pronunciation and should not be divided.

2. Do not cut off one letter.

    UNACCEPTABLE: e·nough   a·gain

3. Cut off prefixes and suffixes.

    PREFIXES: mis·spell   under·estimate   bi·cycle
    SUFFIXES: plen·ti·ful   late·ly   dic·tion·ary
                pro·nun·ci·a·tion (It is best to keep the *a* [or any other syllable with only a vowel] at the end of the line.)

4. Divide between *double letters*.

    be·gin·ning   oc·cur·rence   ex·cel·lent

If the double letter is part of the word before *-ing,* keep the double letters together.

    tell·ing   confess·ing

5. Divide between the parts of a compound word.

    every·where   news·stand   laundry·man

6. If the word already has a hyphen, divide there. It is not acceptable usage to have two hyphens in one word.

    self-satisfied   forty-seven

7. Do not divide names or numbers.

If you are in doubt about how to divide a word at the end of the line, consult a dictionary. Divisions between syllables are marked in the dictionary by dots or accent marks.

Actually, it is best to avoid dividing a word at the end of a line. If a wide margin is left on the right side of the paper, the number of words that need to be divided can be reduced.

inform
informal

In formal writing, it is advisable to avoid informal usages such as the following:

1. Contractions (*I'm, isn't*).

2. Colloquial words such as *kid* for *child, guy* for *man,* or especially slang words such as *chick* for *girl, booze* for *liquor.*

3. Grammatical usages such as:

> the plural *their* to refer to grammatically singular words like *everybody* (*Everybody brought **their** lunch.*)
>
> different *than* for different *from*
>
> who for whom (*a person **who** people admire* for *a person **whom** people admire*)
>
> so for very (*In college there are **so** many interesting activities.*)

Formal writing requires that abbreviations be written out. Numbers consisting of only one or two words (one through one hundred, for example) should also be written out, except in writing of a statistical nature.

intro
introduction

Since the beginning of a composition is the position of greatest emphasis, it is important to write an effective introduction.

An introduction has a double purpose:

First, it lets the reader know what the subject of the composition will be. The introduction usually contains some general treatment of the subject that leads the reader into the specific focus of the composition.

Second, it catches the reader's interest, so that he or she will read on.

There are a number of ways of writing introductions that can hold the reader's attention if they are made interesting enough.

INDEX OF USAGE AND RHETORIC

1. Give a significant anecdote—something that happened (possibly with dialog) that is an illustration of the main point that will be made.

2. Use a striking quotation that is directly related to the central idea of the composition.

3. Include a brief summary statement of the central idea.

4. Give some factual or historical information about the subject of the composition.

5. Ask a question, or a series of questions, the answers to which will be the subject of the composition.

6. State the view that will be opposed in the composition.

7. Give a definition of the key expression in the central idea (for example, *democracy*), telling how it is being interpreted, and possibly how its application is being limited.

The introduction should be in proportion to the length of the composition. It should not be so long that the writer has little time or energy left to develop the main part of the composition.

The introduction should not read as though it was written merely because it is expected in a composition. It should lead naturally into the central idea of the composition. Sometimes it is best to write the introduction after the rest of the composition has been written; by this time a suitable introduction may suggest itself. Also, sometimes what has been written as a first main point may actually be general enough and meaningful enough in terms of the specific subject to serve as an introduction.

neg

negative

Verbs are made negative through the use of *not* placed after an auxiliary.

> POSITIVE: The train has arrived.
> NEGATIVE: The train has not (*or* hasn't) arrived.

If the positive verb has no auxiliary, a form of *do* is added for the negative.

> POSITIVE: The train arrived late.
> NEGATIVE: The train did not (*or* didn't) arrive late.

(See **Verb, 2E,** for more information about making verbs negative.)

Nouns are made negative through the use of *no*.

INDEX OF USAGE AND RHETORIC

POSITIVE: This enterprise requires some money.
NEGATIVE: This enterprise requires *no* money.

No is usually used with *more* for the negative.

He has no more money.

The use of double negatives should be avoided.

UNACCEPTABLE: The children didn't receive no presents this year.
CORRECTION: The children didn't receive any presents this year.
OR: The children received no presents this year.

UNACCEPTABLE: They never go there no more.
CORRECTION: They never go there anymore.
OR: They don't ever go there anymore.

Scarcely and *hardly* are near negatives and should not be used with another negative.

UNACCEPTABLE: They have hardly no business these days.
CORRECTION: They have hardly any business these days.

Note: An acceptable kind of double negative is the combination of *not* plus a word beginning with a negative prefix (usually *un-* or *in-*).

It is *not uncommon* to see tame squirrels in city parks.

Such a combination represents a weakened positive.

A subject containing the word *any*, *every*, or *each* is not generally used with a negative verb.

UNACCEPTABLE: Any student is not allowed in this building.
CORRECTION: No student is allowed in this building.

N

number (of nouns and adjectives)

The following rules about the singular or plural number of nouns and adjectives should be observed.

1. *Nouns*

A. Nouns are regularly made plural by:

adding *-s:* girl – girls
adding *-es:* dish – dishes   wife – wives   lady – ladies
tomato – tomatoes

(See **Spelling** for rules for *-es* plurals.)

23

Other types of plural:

-en added:	child – children		
internal changes:	tooth – teeth	foot – feet	man – men
no change:	deer – deer	means – means	

Foreign plurals:

-is becomes *-es:* crisis – crises
-us becomes *-i:* stimulus – stimuli

Many other foreign words have developed a regular English plural along with the foreign plural.

-um becomes *-a:* memorandum – memoranda (*also* memorandums)
-a becomes *-ae:* formula – formulae (*also* formulas)
-on becomes *-a:* criterion – criteria (*also* criterions)
-eau becomes *-eaux:* bureau – bureaux (*also* bureaus)
-ex, -ix become *-ices:* appendix – appendices (*also* appendixes)

If you are in doubt about the plural of a noun, check the dictionary. If a noun has a plural other than *-s,* the dictionary will give this plural form.

> **B.** The following types of nouns are often used in a noncountable sense. In this use they do not take plural endings. As subjects, they require singular verbs.
>
>> **(1)** Nouns referring to many things that are considered as one unit:
>>
>>> information, furniture, equipment, advice, vocabulary, scenery
>>
>> **(2)** Mass nouns:
>>
>>> *food:*   coffee, sugar
>>> *minerals, materials:*   gold, glass
>>
>> **(3)** Abstract nouns:
>>
>>> beauty, democracy
>>
>> **(4)** Fields of study or work:
>>
>>> music, philosophy, physics, mathematics

Some mass nouns and abstract nouns may be used in a countable sense and therefore may be made plural.

> There are few real *democracies* in the world today. (The plural represents forms of government.)
>
> Oranges and limes are citrus *fruits.* (The plural represents kinds of fruit.)

(See **Article, 9** and **10,** for more information about nouns used in either a noncountable or a countable sense.)

C. A noun after *one of the* is plural.

> One of the tallest buildings in New York is the Empire State Building.

2. Adjectives

Most adjectives do not have plural forms. Exceptions are:

Singular	Plural
this	these
that	those
much	many
little	few
less	fewer (informal *less*)

Much and *little* are used with noncountable nouns.

> much furniture (but many chairs)
> little machinery (but few machines)

(See **Pronoun, 4,** for number in pronouns. Also see **Agreement,** and see **Verb, 5,** for singular or plural forms involved in the agreement between subject and verb.)

par

paragraph development

¶ New paragraph

no ¶ No new paragraph

The paragraph follows many of the same organizational principles of writing that govern the whole composition. Especially important are the principles of unity (establishing the central idea of the paragraph), continuity (connecting the details in the paragraph), and adequate development of the central idea of the paragraph.

Unity

In a properly unified paragraph, all the details in the paragraph are controlled by one central idea, which comes from a point on the outline. Frequently this central idea is stated in one sentence in the paragraph, called the *topic sentence*. Since the beginning of a piece of writing is the place of greatest emphasis, the topic sentence is often the opening sentence of a paragraph. This is especially true in exposition, the kind of discourse that explains, clarifies, defines; this type is the one most commonly used in college texts and in required college writing.

If the opening sentence does not give the complete central idea of a paragraph, it may suggest how the paragraph will be organized in relation to its central idea. It may give part of the main idea, which will be completed by a later sentence. It may also introduce an idea that will be contradicted or qualified by a later idea which really states the writer's main idea. In any case, the opening sentence of a paragraph makes a commitment related to the subject of the paragraph which a writer must follow through.

A second place of emphasis, final position, may also contain an expression of the main idea of a paragraph. The concluding sentence of a paragraph may be merely a restatement of the central idea, it may make a further generalization about the topic, or it may lead into the main idea of the paragraph that follows.

Continuity

There are two rhetorical devices that provide for the smooth flow of ideas in a paragraph as well as in an entire composition. One kind helps to achieve *coherence,* so that sentence is joined to sentence, and paragraph to paragraph. Devices for coherence *point back to what has already been said:* they mark connections with the ideas that precede them.

Some devices that establish coherence by pointing back are repetition of key expressions, pronouns, transitional expressions (such as *therefore, however*), parallel structure (a second logically related idea is placed in the same grammatical structure as the first idea).

The second means of establishing continuity is through the order, or *arrangement,* of the ideas that are presented. This type suggests *a movement forward to what is to follow.* Examples of this kind of movement are time, space, or order of importance.

(More information about continuity is given in **Transition** and **Connection.**)

Adequate paragraph development

The central idea of a paragraph should be supported with sufficient details so that the point of the paragraph is convincing. There are a number of ways of supplying details—for example, comparing or contrasting, giving examples, defining, dividing the subject into several aspects or parts, giving causes or effects. The details should be presented in such a way that their relationship to the main idea of the paragraph is clear. Also, more supporting details should be used for the more important ideas in the composition.

//
parallelism

When items in a sentence are joined equally, we expect them to have the same grammatical structure and to be on the same level of meaning.

> Enjoying ourselves and forgetting about our problems are very important for our mental health.

The following are examples of common types of faulty parallelism.

1. Structures joined by coordinate conjunctions (*and, or,* and sometimes *but*) do not have the same grammatical form.

FAULTY PARALLELISM:	I have always liked *science courses* and *to do experiments.*
CORRECTION:	I have always liked *science courses* and *experiments.* (*And* joins two noun objects after *liked.*)
OR:	I have always liked *to take* science courses and *to do* experiments (*And* joins two infinitive objects after *liked.*)

Most mistakes in parallel structure are of this type.

2. Items in a series do not follow grammatically from the word they are dependent on.

FAULTY PARALLELISM:	Americans want television to inform them about foreign news, domestic news, and entertainment. (*Entertainment* cannot depend on *inform about.*)
CORRECTION:	Americans turn to television for foreign news, domestic news, and entertainment. (All three nouns can be used after *for.*)

3. A verb used after *than* (for comparison, preference) does not have the same form as the verb before *than.*

FAULTY PARALLELISM:	It is better *to repeat* a noun than *making* an ambiguous statement.
CORRECTION:	It is better *to repeat* a noun than *to make* an ambiguous statement.

4. Items joined by *and* are logically on different levels of meaning.

INDEX OF USAGE AND RHETORIC

FAULTY PARALLELISM: English is simpler than Korean because it doesn't have as many delicate or polite expressions and it has only 26 letters in the alphabet.

CORRECTION: English is simpler than Korean for two reasons. First, English has only 26 letters in the alphabet. Second, it does not have as many delicate or polite expressions. (The two different types of reasons originally joined by *and* have been separated into two sentences to give more "space" between them.)

In formal writing, structure words referring to items in a series (prepositions, articles, auxiliaries) are often repeated for the sake of clarity.

Nowadays, a boy can meet a girl anywhere—*at* the theater, *at* the beach, *at* school. (By putting in each preposition in such a sentence, the writer can make sure that the same preposition is indeed the correct one for each of the parallel items.)

Sometimes sentences containing items joined by a coordinate conjunction do not really violate the requirements of grammatical parallelism, but they can be improved if both parts are made parallel.

POOR: The ideal situation for a student is to study something that he likes, but at the same time preparation for his economic future is very important. (The two parts joined by *but* seem to be about two different things.)

IMPROVED: The ideal situation for a student is to study something *that* he likes but *that* will also prepare him for his economic future. (The two parts now are about the same subject (*that* representing *something*.)

Parallel structure is required not only for items in sentences but for items on outlines. The most common fault is to use both nouns and verbs together in the outline.

UNACCEPTABLE:
  I. *Decision* to travel abroad
  II. *Preparing* for the trip
  III. *The trip* on the plane
  IV. *Arriving* in the foreign country

This outline may be corrected by making all the items either verbs or nouns.

All Items Are Nouns:
  I. Decision to travel abroad
  II. Preparations for the trip
  III. The trip on the plane
  IV. Arrival in the foreign country

All Items Are Verbs:
  I. Deciding to travel abroad
  II. Preparing for the trip
  III. Traveling on the plane
  IV. Arriving in the foreign country.

INDEX OF USAGE AND RHETORIC

prep
preposition

The most common prepositions of time and place are given below.

1. *Common prepositions of time*

    ON   With days (especially dates or days of the week) (*on* may be omitted):

    > He will arrive (on) January 15.

    AT   With *noon, night, midnight:*

    > The train arrives at noon.

    With the time of day:

    > The train arrives at five o'clock.

    SINCE   Gives the beginning of a time, which often continues into the present (usually expressed as a date, or a point of time):

    > I have lived here since 1970.

    FOR   Gives the duration (length) of a time, often expressed as a quantity (*for* may be omitted):

    > I have lived here (for) twelve years.

2. *Common prepositions of place*

    IN   Inside some place that is contained:

    > in the room, in the drawer

    AT   Some general location:

    > at the corner of Hollywood and Vine Streets

    For an address:

    AT   With the street number:

    > at 500 Fifth Avenue

    ON   With the street only:

    > on Fifth Avenue

    With the verb *arrive:*

    IN   A large place (a country, a state):

    > in Argentina, in Massachusetts

INDEX OF USAGE AND RHETORIC

AT   A small location:

    at the airport, at the station, at the store

For a city, *in,* sometimes *at,* is used.

The following *faults in the use of prepositions* should be avoided.

1. Repeating or including a preposition unnecessarily.

UNACCEPTABLE:	The house *in* which he lives *in* is very large.
CORRECTION:	The house *in* which he lives is very large.
OR:	The house which he lives *in* is very large.
OR:	The house he lives *in* is very large.

Because *where* often equals a preposition plus *which* (*in which* equals *where,* for example), the preposition may be superfluous.

UNACCEPTABLE:	The house where he lives *in* is very large.
CORRECTION:	The house where he lives is very large.

2. Omitting a required preposition after an infinitive.

UNACCEPTABLE:	We'd like to have some music to dance.
CORRECTION:	We'd like to have some music to dance *to.* (The actual object of *to* is *music.*)

3. Not adding *the* to *of* after pronouns referring to *parts.* Words like *most, many, some,* and *none* should be followed either by *of the* for specific reference or by no preposition at all for general reference.

SPECIFIC REFERENCE:	*Most of the* students in the class passed the examination.
GENERAL REFERENCE:	*Most* students study hard in the university.
UNACCEPTABLE:	*Most of* Japanese people have a vacation from work during the New Year's holiday.
CORRECTION:	*Most* Japanese people have a vacation from work during the New Year's holiday.

Note: After *all* and *half,* the word *of* may be omitted, but *the* must be used.

    All (*or* half) *of the* students passed the examination.
OR: All (*or* half) *the* students passed the examination.

4. Using *of* before a word of quantity.

UNACCEPTABLE:	About 1,000,000 *of* people live in this town.
CORRECTION:	About 1,000,000 people live in this town.

5. In phrases joined by *and,* using one preposition for both phrases, although each phrase requires its own preposition.

INDEX OF USAGE AND RHETORIC

UNACCEPTABLE: I have always viewed the Filipinos as true lovers and fighters for freedom.

CORRECTION: I have always viewed the Filipinos as true lovers of and fighters for freedom.

6. Using the wrong prepositions in the following expressions:

based *on*	*in* other words
be composed *of*	look *at*
consist *of*	look forward *to* (+ the *-ing* form of the verb)
depend *on* (or *upon*)	*on* the contrary
difference *between*	the same *as*
interested *in*	wait *for*
listen *to*	*on* the other hand

After the verb *prefer,* the preposition *to* should be used for the second choice.

I prefer jazz *to* rock music.
Most people prefer paying a fine *to* going to prison.

But if an infinitive is used after *prefer,* the second choice should be introduced by *rather than.*

Most people prefer to pay a fine *rather than* (to) go to prison.

7. With verbs of speaking, using the wrong preposition, or incorrectly adding or omitting a preposition. The following list gives the correct forms after verbs of speaking.

discuss something *with* someone

describe
explain
mention   something *to* someone
say
suggest

After *tell,* the speaker may use either the same form as above: tell something *to* someone, or tell someone something.

speak	*to* / *with*	someone	*about* / *of*[4]	something
OR:				
speak	*about* / *of*[4]	something	*with*	someone
talk	*to* / *with*	someone	*about* / *of*[4]	something
OR:				
talk	*about* / *of*[4]	something	*with*	someone

[4] *Of* is less commonly used with these verbs.

INDEX OF USAGE AND RHETORIC

Ask or *answer* are not followed by a preposition for a person or a thing.

ask
answer } someone something

8. Using a preposition incorrectly after certain verbs when no preposition is required. Confusion arises because some of these verbs have synonyms that require prepositions.

Verb with No Preposition	Synonym with Preposition
attend (a school)	go to (a school)
discuss (a subject)	talk about (a subject)
enter (a building)	go into or in (a building)
marry (someone)	get married to (someone)

pro

pronoun

The following usages with regard to pronouns should be observed.

1. The object form of a personal pronoun is required when the pronoun is the object of a verb or a preposition.

> She gave *me* (*him, us, them*) a good book.
> She gave a good book to *me* (*him, us, them*).

A pronoun object after *and* should have object form.

> They invited my wife and *me* to the conference. (Both *wife* and *me* are objects of the verb *invited*.)

2. In an adjective clause, the relative pronoun *who* (*whom, whose*) is used for a person, *which* for a thing.

> The person *who* told me the story is a good friend of mine.
> The thing *which* impressed me the most was his honesty.

In formal usage, *whom* is required when it is the object of a verb or a preposition.

> The person *whom* (informal: *who*) you should see is Dr. Jones.[5]

In informal English, the pronoun object in an adjective clause may be omitted if there is no comma before it (restrictive clause). (For the punctua-

---

[5] The object form *whom* is required in formal English not only in adjective clauses but in direct questions (*Whom* should I see?) and in indirect questions (Please tell me *whom* I should see).

tion of adjective clauses, see **Punctuation, 2B,** and Grammar Review and Practice, Unit 3.)

> The person you should see is Dr. Jones.

That is an alternative for *who* or *which* in a restrictive clause.

> The thing *that* impressed me the most was his honesty.

3. The pronouns *there* and *it* may be used as "empty" words that merely fill subject position.

> *There* + a form of *be* + a *noun:*

> There are several *reasons* why the plan didn't succeed.

> *It* + a form of *be* + an *adjective:*

> It's very *pleasant* in this hotel.

The use of *it* in subject position is quite common, especially in sentences that contain a long subject and a short predicate.

> It's very important *to take care of that matter at once.* (= To take care of that matter at once is very important.)
>
> It is well known that he has never done an honest day's work. (= That he has never done an honest day's work is well known.)

The following pronoun faults should be avoided.[6]

1. Using a pronoun that can refer to either of two preceding nouns.

> UNACCEPTABLE: Whenever John is able to help his brother financially, *he* is very happy.

In such a sentence, it is better to repeat the noun than to make an ambiguous statement.

> CORRECTION: Whenever John is able to help his brother financially, John (*or* his brother) is very happy.

It is not considered good usage to place a word in parentheses after a pronoun in order to clarify its meaning.

> UNACCEPTABLE: Whenever John is able to help his brother, he (John) is very happy.
>
> CORRECTION: Whenever John is able to help his brother, John is very happy.

---

[6] Some of the examples of pronoun faults have been taken from Marcella Frank, *Modern English: A Practical Reference Guide* (Englewood Cliffs, N.J.: Prentice-Hall, 1972).

2. Using a pronoun (usually *this* or *it*) that does not refer back to a specific noun. Its reference must be inferred.

> UNACCEPTABLE: My father is an engineer. *This* is a profession I admire very much. (An engineer is a person, not a profession.)
>
> CORRECTION: My father is an engineer. Engineering is a profession I admire very much.
>
> UNACCEPTABLE: If students are forced to study the classics, *it* won't do them any good.
>
> CORRECTION: Forcing students to study the classics won't do them any good.
>
> OR: It won't do students any good to force them to study the classics.

3. Using *this* or *that* to refer too far back to some part of the preceding sentence(s).

> UNACCEPTABLE: Stores sell many more toys than they did a few generations ago. *This* deprives children of the pleasure of making their own toys. (How far back does *this* go?)

In this sentence, the word *this* requires an accompanying expression that makes its reference more specific.

> CORRECTION: This abundance of ready-made toys deprives children of the pleasure of making their own toys.

4. Using a plural pronoun to refer to a singular noun, or vice versa.

> UNACCEPTABLE: The *student* must be made to understand how each lesson can be of value to *them*.

This fault often occurs in a general statement, which can use a singular or a plural noun to represent a class (*the student* or *students*).

> CORRECTION: *Students* must be made to understand how each lesson can be of value to *them*.

There is a very common tendency in informal English to prefer the plural *they* to refer to the grammatically singular *everybody* or *everyone* in order to avoid using the required *he* or the more awkward *he or she*. As a matter of fact, sometimes *they* is the only possible word to use, as in: *Is everybody here? Yes, they are.*

5. Changing the pronoun used to make general statements.

> UNACCEPTABLE: *We* should obey the law at all times. If *you* don't, *you* may have to pay a fine or go to prison.
>
> CORRECTION: *We* should obey the law at all times. If *we* don't, *we* may have to pay a fine or go to prison. (Or *you* may be used in both sentences.)

INDEX OF USAGE AND RHETORIC

6. Using *which* with indefinite reference.

UNACCEPTABLE:	He is a graduate of one of the Ivy League schools, *which* should open many doors to him. (*Which* refers back to the whole statement that precedes it.)
CORRECTION:	The fact that he is a graduate of one of the Ivy League schools should open many doors to him.

Although indefinite *which* is common in informal English, such use should be avoided in formal English.

7. Using *it* or *they* loosely as an impersonal subject while the real subject precedes it in a prepositional phrase.

UNACCEPTABLE:	In the newspaper *it* says that the concert was canceled.
CORRECTION:	The newspaper says that the concert was canceled.
UNACCEPTABLE:	At the university *they* require an examination for all entering freshmen.
CORRECTION:	The university requires an examination for all entering freshmen.

8. Adding an unnecessary pronoun.

UNACCEPTABLE:	My friend, *he* told me the whole story.
CORRECTION:	My friend told me the whole story.

A pronoun is sometimes repeated incorrectly in an adjective clause.

UNACCEPTABLE REPEATED *SUBJECT*:	The teacher who *he* had the greatest influence on me was my English teacher.
CORRECTION:	The teacher who had the greatest influence on me was my English teacher.
UNACCEPTABLE REPEATED *OBJECT*:	The subject which I liked *it* the best in school was English.
CORRECTION:	The subject which I liked the best in school was English.

Sometimes an unacceptable pronoun is used as an object of an infinitive.

UNACCEPTABLE:	Some water is not fit to drink *it*.
CORRECTION:	Some water is not fit to drink. (*Water* is the real object of *drink*.)

9. Placing many *it*'s close together.

CARELESS:	We like *it* very much in this hotel. *It*'s wonderful to relax in *its* comfortable atmosphere. *It*'s possible we'll stay in *it* again on our next vacation.

INDEX OF USAGE AND RHETORIC

CORRECTION: We like this hotel very much. Its relaxing and comfortable atmosphere is wonderful. We may stay here again on our next vacation.

10. Using the pronoun *what* instead of *that* in an adjective clause, especially after a pronoun like *all* or *everything*.

UNACCEPTABLE: All *what* I need now is some rest.
CORRECTION: All *that* I need now is some rest.

11. Using the singular pronoun *another* (= *an* + *other*) as a plural.

UNACCEPTABLE: Many people in my country have to emigrate to *another* countries.
CORRECTION: Many people in my country have to emigrate to *other* countries.

Note: *Other* is generally used with a plural noun.

Some people like the country; *other* people like the seashore.

The other is singular if it represents the second of two. *The others* represents two or more.

One sister has gone to college; *the other* (of two sisters) has not.
One sister has gone to college; *the others* (of two or more sisters) have not.

Others is the plural form of *other* when the word is used alone.

Some people like the country; *others* (= other people) like the seashore.

12. Confusing *it* and *there* in subject position.

UNACCEPTABLE: *It* is too much pollution in big cities.
CORRECTION: *There* is too much pollution in big cities.

P

punctuation

This section on punctuation deals mainly with specific marks of punctuation that are related to sentence structure. However, two warnings about the use of punctuation in general need to be made first.

1. No punctuation should be used at the beginning of a line. (Exceptions are quotation marks and parentheses, which must appear directly around the words they refer to.)

2. No more than one end mark of punctuation should be used. The doubling or tripling of periods, question marks, or exclamation points should be avoided in English.

INDEX OF USAGE AND RHETORIC

The information about punctuation that follows is presented under these headings:

1. Commas in sentences with introductory, final grammatical elements

2. Commas in sentences with interrupting elements

3. Commas, semicolons in combined independent sentences

4. Commas in a series

5. Commas and quotation marks in direct speech

6. Other uses of punctuation for sentence structure (colon, semicolon, dash)

7. Unacceptable commas (including run-on sentences)

8. Unacceptable semicolons

1. *Commas in sentences with introductory or final grammatical elements*

A comma is generally used after an introductory element, especially if this element is long or if the writer would normally pause at this point in speech. A comma after a short introductory element is optional.

WORDS:	*Finally(,)*[7] they were able to take their trip around the world.
PHRASES:	*As a matter of fact,* they went on the trip sooner than they had expected.
CLAUSES:	*Before they left,*[8] their friends gave them a big party.

There are some types of introductory phrases that require commas.

Hoping to see as much as possible, they planned their itinerary carefully. (participial phrase)

Happy to be leaving at last, they boarded the plane with great anticipation. (adjective phrase)

The weather causing no problems, they had a comfortable flight. (absolute construction)

Final elements are less likely to be set off by commas, especially those indicating time. However, as with introductory elements, a pause in speech determines whether a comma will be used.

WORDS:	They realized their dream *unexpectedly.*
PHRASES:	They realized their dream *in an unexpected manner.*
CLAUSES:	Their wish came true *when they unexpectedly inherited some money.*

---

[7] The parentheses around a mark of punctuation indicates that the punctuation is optional.

[8] The comma is required after the short introductory element in this sentence to avoid a temporary misreading as: *Before they left their friends.*

The same elements that require commas at the beginning of the sentence also require commas when they appear at the end of the sentence.

> They planned their itinerary carefully, *hoping to see as much as possible.* (participial phrase)
> They boarded the plane with great anticipation, *happy to be leaving at last.* (adjective phrase).
> They had a comfortable flight, *the weather causing no problems.* (absolute construction)

2. *Commas in sentences with interrupting elements*

Since interrupting elements are regarded as parenthetic, commas are placed on *both sides* of the elements.

A. Adverbial elements

WORDS: His father, *fortunately,* was very rich.
PHRASES: His father, *as a matter of fact,* was very rich.
CLAUSES: His father, *as I've been told,* was very rich.

If a short word or phrase is felt to be closely related to the rest of the sentence, the commas may be omitted.

> Their wish *finally* came true.

B. Nonrestrictive structures

An adjective structure that follows a noun may either narrow down (that is, restrict) the reference of the noun, or it may only add more information about the noun without identifying it further. *Those structures that do not identify their nouns are considered nonrestrictive and require commas.*

Note the difference in punctuation in the following sentences.

Restrictive—No Commas	Nonrestrictive—Commas on Both Sides
Land which is surrounded by water is an island. (The noun *land* is a general [class] word. It is identified by *which is surrounded by water.*)	*Manhattan,* which is surrounded by water, is an island. (The noun *Manhattan* is already identified by name, so *which is surrounded by water* does not limit its identity further.)

The same punctuation rule applies to participial phrases, which may be considered shortened forms of *who* or *which* clauses.

RESTRICTIVE: Land *surrounded by water* is an island.
NONRESTRICTIVE: Manhattan, *surrounded by water,* is an island.

INDEX OF USAGE AND RHETORIC

Other shortened forms of nonrestrictive *who* or *which* clauses also require commas if the nouns they refer to are already identified by name.

The Palace, *a very expensive restaurant,* serves only the best food.
The Palace, *famous for its fine food,* is a very expensive restaurant.

The nonrestrictive phrase can also be moved to the beginning of the sentence.

Surrounded by water, Manhattan is an island.

3. *Commas and semicolons in combined independent sentences*

A. Comma

The boy was sick, *so* he didn't go to school.	When connectives like *so, and, but,* and *or* (coordinate conjunctions) join sentences, a comma is used. The comma may be omitted if both sentences are short.

B. Semicolon

The boy was sick; he didn't go to school.	No connective joins the sentences. Sometimes two sentences are written as one because the writer feels there is a relationship between them. In this case they are joined by a semicolon.
The boy was sick; *therefore*(,) he didn't go to school.	Adverbials like *therefore, however, otherwise, moreover* (conjunctive adverbs) can connect the sentences. These adverbials may take other positions in the second part of the sentence: The boy was sick; he *therefore* didn't go to school. Note that *the semicolon remains in the position where the period might have been written.*

4. *Commas in a series* (*with* **and, or**)

Items in a series of three or more are separated by commas.

The advertising company is preparing a television program that can appeal to men, women(,) or children.

INDEX OF USAGE AND RHETORIC

> In a democracy, people have the right to speak freely, to assemble without government interference(,) and to worship in the religion of their choice.

The comma before *and* or *or* is optional.
   If *and* or *or* is omitted, the comma must be used.

> The Constitution guarantees freedom of speech, assembly, religion.

5. *Commas and quotation marks in direct speech*

Quotation marks are used around the words of direct speech, and commas separate these words from phrases like *he said, they asked.*

> Someone in the audience shouted, "That's a crazy idea."
> She asked her husband, "Why can't we move to a better neighborhood?"

Note the following:

- the comma after *shouted* and *husband.*
- the position of the quotation marks—both the opening and closing quotes are near the top of the letters.
- the position of the final period and the question mark—these are *inside* the closing quotation mark.
- the use of a capital letter for the first word of the direct speech.

Phrases like *he said,* and *they asked* are also set off with commas when they appear in the middle or at the end of the quoted speech.

> "Why," she asked, "can't we move to a better neighborhood?"
> "That's a crazy idea," someone in the audience shouted.

6. *Other uses of punctuation for sentence structure*

A. Colon

The colon is a formal mark of punctuation that anticipates or explains what follows.

> The following countries make up the major part of Great Britain: England, Wales, Scotland.
>
> In a democracy, the civil rights of the individual are protected: the law guarantees freedom of speech, freedom of assembly, and freedom of religion. (In less formal usage, a semicolon can appear in such a sentence instead of the colon.)

B. Semicolon

The chief use of the semicolon is to permit two independent sentences to be joined into one (see **Punctuation, 3,** for examples). The semicolon replaces the period that separates the sentences. To make sentences easier to read, the writer should avoid combining long sentences with a semicolon or using more than one semicolon in a sentence.

Another use of the semicolon is to mark a sharper break than a comma would.

> **(1)** A semicolon separates fairly long items in a list.
>
> I have two main objectives in going to the university: (1) to prepare for a professional career; (2) to increase my knowledge about the world and the people in it.
>
> The 1970 Census gives the following figures for the three largest metropolitan areas in the United States: New York, 11,575,740; Los Angeles, 7,032,075; Chicago, 6,978,947. (Note that the semicolon is especially necessary if there are already commas with the items on the list.)
>
> **(2)** A semicolon replaces a comma before a coordinate conjunction (especially *and* or *but*) that joins two sentences if each part of the sentence is long or already has commas within it.
>
> They have already visited New York, Boston, and Washington in the East; and, as far as we know, the next cities on their itinerary are in the Midwest.
>
> **C. Dash**
>
> The dash marks a sharp interruption in the structure of a sentence.
>
> In some parts of the world—this is hard to believe—many people live to be well over a hundred years.

In informal writing the dash often becomes an "all-purpose" mark of punctuation that replaces the comma, the semicolon, or the colon. However, the dash should be used sparingly in formal writing.

7. *Unacceptable commas*

> **A.** A comma should not be used before *and* or *or* connecting *two* words or phrases.
>
> > UNACCEPTABLE: He likes to eat a little bread, and cheese before he goes to bed. (Two nouns—bread, cheese—are joined by *and*.)
> > The democratic way of life offers people freedom of speech, and gives them the opportunity to make full use of their abilities. (Two verbs—offers, gives—are joined by *and*.)

However, the comma is acceptable if *and* or *or* joins two independent sentences.

B. A comma should not be placed between the subject–verb–complement center of the sentence.

(1) Between a subject and a predicate.

UNACCEPTABLE: The fact that there are a few exceptions, does not disprove his theory.

The democratic way of life, provides freedom of speech and freedom of the press.

Such an unnecessary comma often appears at the end of a restrictive adjective clause, which should not be punctuated with commas at all.

UNACCEPTABLE: People who love their freedom, are willing to fight for it.

(2) Between a verb and its complement.

The most common fault here is to place a comma between the verb and the word that introduces a noun-clause object.

UNACCEPTABLE: Everyone in the room said, that he was guilty.
I don't know, why he did it.

C. An interrupting adverbial element that has a comma on one side should have a comma on the other side as well.

UNACCEPTABLE: Astrology as everyone knows, deals with the influence of the heavenly bodies on human lives. (This sentence requires another comma before *as*.)

They in fact, help each other. (Since commas around this short adverbial expression are optional, the sentence can be corrected by placing another comma before *in* or omitting the comma after *fact*.)

D. A comma should not be used between two sentences that have been joined into one with either no connecting word or with an adverbial such as *therefore, however, for example, in other words*. Such unacceptable sentences are called *run-on* sentences.

RUN-ON SENTENCES: The people in my country are friendly and honest, a visitor doesn't have to be afraid of anything.
I will have to read more in college, consequently I will improve my reading skill.

Sometimes even the comma is omitted in a combined sentence.

RUN-ON SENTENCES: Manhattan is an unusual island it's close enough to the East Coast to be connected by several bridges.

INDEX OF USAGE AND RHETORIC

The verbs in Portuguese have endings therefore we do not need to write down the personal pronouns.

Run-on sentences can be corrected by placing a semicolon or a period where the two sentences come together.

E. A comma should not be put after a conjunction.

(1) After a coordinate conjunction (*and, but, or, nor, for*):

UNACCEPTABLE: But, the reason I am studying at the university is that I want to understand the world and my society.

(2) After a subordinate conjunction (especially *because, although*):

UNACCEPTABLE: I do not believe in astrology although, I find it very interesting.

8. *Unacceptable semicolons*

Most unacceptable semicolons cut off a part of a sentence instead of joining two sentences into one. Such faults can be corrected by *changing the semicolon to a comma.*

The following are examples of the most common types of final elements that are cut off with semicolons instead of commas.

His secretary has worked overtime for several days; hoping to finish all the work she had to do.
The transit workers in the city went on strike; the result being that many people could not get to their places of employment.
Some people get most of their news from the newspapers; while (*or whereas*) others get their information mainly from television.
I want an education that will broaden my outlook on life; an education that will help me face the world in a more mature way.
Television has had a profound influence on American society; both beneficial and detrimental.
Women, like most men, have desires for complete lives; which usually means having loving families and satisfaction in their careers. (In this sentence, if the indefinite *which* is replaced by *this*, a word that is not grammatically dependent on what precedes it, the semicolon may be retained.)

Sometimes the same final elements that are cut off unacceptably with semicolons are separated even more sharply from their sentences with periods. The final part that has been cut off and placed in another sentence is usually labeled a *fragment.* (See **Fragment**.)

Other types of misuse of the semicolon are:

A. Using a semicolon instead of a colon to anticipate a list.

INDEX OF USAGE AND RHETORIC

UNACCEPTABLE: Nowadays there are plenty of professional schools; business, engineering, medical schools.
CORRECTION: (Use a colon after *professional schools*.)

B. Using a semicolon instead of a comma or no punctuation after an expression like *for example* or *such as*.

UNACCEPTABLE: For the reasons I have already given, such as; the woman's career, the need for self-fulfillment, I believe the woman should have the right to make her own choice.
CORRECTION: (Remove the semicolon after *such as*.)

repet

repetitious

The repetition of words or ideas should be avoided, except where it is needed to provide connections between ideas or to give additional emphasis to a point being made.

It is true that sometimes the repetition of certain words can be very effective, as in Lincoln's famous phrase about government "of the people, by the people, for the people." At other times the repetition of structure words helps to make parallelism clear:

> The newly elected president promised *to* provide jobs for all, *to* reduce the rate of inflation, and *to* set up a national health system.

Many times, however, the repetition is unnecessary and monotonous.

REPETITIOUS: I really like my work, and I enjoy doing it, because I work with very friendly people.
IMPROVED: I really like (or enjoy) my job, because I work with very friendly people.

REPETITIOUS: When I was a child, a university education was supposed to be the realization of a dream but later I realized that my university education was not everything it was supposed to be.
IMPROVED: When I was a child, I dreamed of having a university education, but later I discovered that such an education was not everything it was supposed to be. (The removal of the repeated words makes this sentence less wordy.)

The use of more than one expression to state the same relationship should be avoided.

INDEX OF USAGE AND RHETORIC

like, for instance
and also
but however

In a conclusion that summarizes the main points of a composition, these ideas should be restated in another way, not only to avoid being repetitious, but to make the ideas more emphatic.

SS

sentence structure

Many of the faults in sentence structure occur when one of the required elements in the subject–verb–complement pattern is omitted or is used incorrectly in a sentence. (See the chart of sentence patterns at the end of this section if you are having problems with these sentence elements.)

1. *Omission of the subject*

UNACCEPTABLE: Malaysia is situated in Southeast Asia is a small, independent country.

CORRECTION: Malaysia, *which* is situated in Southeast Asia, is a small, independent country. (By omitting the first *is*, we can use a structure for which the subject is not needed: *Malaysia, situated in Southeast Asia, is a small, independent country.*)

Related to this problem of the omission of the subject is the omission of *it* or *there,* which merely fills subject position while the true subject comes after the verb in the predicate.

IT OMITTED: Is necessary to leave right away.
CORRECTION: *It* is necessary to leave right away.

THERE OMITTED: In a democracy must be a multi-party system.
CORRECTION: In a democracy *there* must be a multi-party system.

2. *Omission of the verb*

UNACCEPTABLE: It has a large population, more than one million, but it not as noisy and dirty as New York City.

CORRECTION: It has a large population, more than one million, but it *is* not as noisy and dirty as New York City.

3. *Omission of the object*

Some verbs cannot be used without objects. Examples of such verbs are *enjoy, love, marry,* and *admire.*

45

INDEX OF USAGE AND RHETORIC

UNACCEPTABLE: If you visit my country, you will enjoy very much.
CORRECTION: If you visit my country, you will enjoy *it* very much.

4. *Incorrect structure used as a subject*

   A. The object in a prepositional phrase is incorrectly used as the subject.

   UNACCEPTABLE: Right now in Colombia has a serious problem with unemployment.
   CORRECTION: Right now *Colombia* has a serious problem with unemployment.

   B. An adverbial clause is incorrectly used as the subject.

   UNACCEPTABLE: When children are neglected in the home may cause them to have emotional problems.
   CORRECTION: When (*or* if) children are neglected in the home, they may have emotional problems.
   OR: The neglect of children in the home may cause them to have emotional problems.

5. *Incorrect phrase used as an object*

A number of verbs can take objects that have subject–verb–complement elements within them. With such verbs there may be choices for the form of these subject–verb–complement elements:

   Their teacher asked *that the students come to class on time.*
   OR: Their teacher asked *the students to come to class on time.*

However, with other verbs, this choice of forms for object phrases is not possible.

   UNACCEPTABLE: I suggest (*or* recommend) *you to go there.*
   CORRECTION: I suggest (*or* recommend) *that you go there.*

SUMMARY OF SENTENCE STRUCTURES

This summary of sentence structures expands some of the information in the Grammar Review and Practice section in order to draw attention to the subject–verb–complement elements in sentences and to point out how these elements may be coordinated, modified, or reduced.

INDEX OF USAGE AND RHETORIC

1. *Sentence patterns*

Subject	Verb	Complement (completes the statement made by the verb)
The girl	laughed.	—— (no complement)
John	loves	the girl. (object)
Einstein	was	a genius. (subjective complement—noun)
Einstein	was	brilliant. (subjective complement—adjective)

Some verbs take two complements.

		First Complement	Second Complement
John	gave	the girl (indirect object)	flowers. (direct object)
People	consider	Einstein (direct object)	a genius. (objective complement—noun)
People	consider	Einstein (direct object)	brilliant. (objective complement—adjective)

The elements in the basic sentence pattern may be expanded by modifiers.

ADJECTIVE: Her *red* hair attracted him.

ADVERB: She dresses *conservatively*.

PREPOSITIONAL PHRASE: The girl *with the red hair* is beautiful.

She dresses *in a conservative manner*.

Each element in the basic sentence pattern, as well as each modifier, can be multiplied by the use of the coordinates *and, (n)or,* and less frequently *but*.

Men, women, or *children* can enjoy this electronic game. (multiple subject)
He *shaved* and *dressed* quickly. (multiple verb)
She was *beautiful* but *dumb*. (multiple complement)

2. *Combinations of sentence patterns*

Sentence patterns can be joined in several ways, with each part called a "clause."

47

A. Two sentence patterns can be joined so that they are equal grammatically (*independent clauses*).

Independent Clause	Independent Clause
He was very tired	; he couldn't finish his work.
The weather is bad now	, and the weatherman predicts snow.
Television can be beneficial	; however, some programs are unsuitable for children.

B. Two sentence patterns can be joined so that one is subordinate to the other as an adverbial modifier (*adverbial clause*).

Independent (Main) Clause	Dependent (Subordinate) Clause
The workers are asking for a raise	because the cost of living has gone up.
She turns on the radio	while she is doing the housework.[9]

Such subordinate clauses may also appear at the beginning of the sentence.

Because the cost of living has gone up, the workers are asking for a raise.

C. One sentence pattern *can be incorporated within* the subject or complement element of a main clause as a modifier (*adjective*, or *relative, clause*).

The man *who invented the telephone* was Alexander Graham Bell.

The main clause is *The man was Alexander Graham Bell.* The clause incorporated within the subject is *who invented the telephone.*

D. One sentence pattern can act as the subject or complement element in a main clause (*noun clause*).

The police wondered *who had committed the crime.*

The entire clause *who had committed the crime* is the complement (object) of the verb *wondered.*

3. *Reduction of sentence patterns within sentences*

A. Subject–verb–complement elements or their modifiers can be reduced so that the verb becomes an *-ing* or *-ed* participle, or the infinitive with *to*. Also, an "understood" subject may be omitted.

---

[9] In some subordinate clauses, the subject and a form of *be* may be omitted (but are "understood"): *She turns on the radio while doing the housework.*

GERUND PHRASE:	They enjoyed *meeting their new neighbors.* (*Meeting their new neighbors* is a complement reduced from *They met their new neighbors.*)
PARTICIPIAL PHRASE:	The houses *damaged by the storm* are being rebuilt. (*Damaged by the storm* is a modifier reduced from *The houses were damaged by the storm.*)
INFINITIVE PHRASE:	We expect *to see them again soon.* (*To see them again soon* is a complement reduced from *We will see them again soon.*)
ABSOLUTE CONSTRUCTION:	*The bus drivers being on strike,* we had to take a taxi. (*The bus drivers being on strike* is an adverbial modifier reduced from *The bus drivers were on strike.*)

B. The subject-verb-complement can be reduced so that only the complement remains.

APPOSITIVE NOUN PHRASE:	Mr. Jones, *a prominent lawyer,* will represent her in court. (*A prominent lawyer* is reduced from *Mr. Jones is a prominent lawyer.*)
APPOSITIVE ADJECTIVE PHRASE:	The hostess, *angry at her husband's rude behavior,* apologized to their guests. (*Angry at her husband's rude behavior* is reduced from *The hostess was angry at her husband's rude behavior.*)

All the dependent clauses and phrases that have been given in 2. and 3. above can also be coordinated with words like *and* and *or*.

CLAUSE:	The police didn't know *who had committed the crime,* or *how it was done.*
PHRASE:	They enjoyed *meeting their new neighbors* and *discussing mutual problems.*

sp
spelling

This section on spelling includes:

1. Spelling rules for *ie* and *ei* words
2. Spelling rules for adding final elements
3. Spelling changes in prefixes before certain letters
4. Word pairs often confused because of similarities in sound
5. 160 frequently misspelled words

INDEX OF USAGE AND RHETORIC

1. *Spelling rules for* ie *and* ei *words*

    A. Use *ie* when the letters have the sound of *ee* (as in *eat*).

          achievement, piece, chief, belief
    EXCEPTIONS: 1. after *c,* use *ei:* receive, deceit
          2. seize, (n)either, leisure, weird

    B. Use *ei* when the letters have other sounds than *ee.*

         weight, height, foreign, their
    EXCEPTION: friend

2. *Spelling rules for adding final elements*

    A. Adding *-es* rather than *-s.*

    (1) Add *-es* to nouns and verbs ending in sibilant sounds—*s, z, ch, sh, x.*

    glasses, buzzes, teaches, dishes, mixes

    (2) Add *-es* to nouns and verbs ending in *y* preceded by a consonant; the *y* changes to *i.*

       babies, carries
    BUT: enjoys, monkeys (*y* is preceded by a vowel)

    (3) Add *-es* to some nouns ending in *o.*

    heroes, potatoes

    Other nouns ending in *o* may take either *-s* or *-es.*

    cargoes or cargos, volcanoes or volcanos.

    (Check the dictionary if you are not sure whether *-s* or *-es* is required with such nouns.)

    B. Doubling final consonants before added syllables *beginning with vowels.*

    Double the consonant if:

     the word ends in *one* consonant preceded by *one* vowel, and the stress is on the syllable where the doubling might take place.

    One-syllable word: plán + ed = plánned
             hót + er = hótter
    Two-syllable word: omít + ing = omítting
             occúr + ence = occúrrence
         but: prefér + ence = préference (the stress shifts to the first syllable)

INDEX OF USAGE AND RHETORIC

C. Dropping or keeping silent *e* before added syllables.

(1) Drop the *e* before a vowel.

advertise + ing = advertising
arrive + al = arrival
noise + y = noisy (for this rule, the adjective ending *y* is treated as a vowel)

Exception: When adjective suffixes beginning with *a, o, u* are added to words ending in *ce* or *ge,* the *e* is kept in order to prevent a change in pronunciation.

noticeable, changeable

(2) Keep the *e* before a consonant.

advertise + ment = advertisement
care + ful = careful
entire + ly = entirely

Exceptions: In a few nouns ending in *-ment,* the *e* is kept in British English.

judgement, abridgement

The *e* is dropped before *th.*

width, ninth, fifth

In words ending in *-ple, -ble,* or *-tle,* the *le* is dropped before *ly.*

simply, possibly, subtly

D. Changing final *y* to *i* before added syllables.

(1) Change *y* to *i* before a vowel.

mystery + ous = mysterious
marry + age = marriage
easy + er = easier

(2) Change *y* to *i* before a consonant.

happy + ness = happiness
glory + fy = glorify
beauty + ful = beautiful
easy + ly = easily

3. *Spelling changes in prefixes before certain letters*

AD = *to, at, toward*

ac + c   accelerate, accidental, accommodate, accumulate, accustom

INDEX OF USAGE AND RHETORIC

ac + q	acquaint, acquiesce, acquire, acquisition, acquittal
af + f	affectation, affidavit, affiliate, affluence, affront
ag + g	aggrandize, aggregate, aggressor
al + l	allegiance, allergy, alleviate, allocate, ally
an + n	annex, annihilate, annulment, announcement
ap + p	appreciate, approximate, apparatus, appendix, applause
ar + r	arraign, arrangement, arrest, arrival, arrogant, arrears
as + s	assignment, assimilate, assistance, association, assumption
at + t	attainment, attempt, attorney, attendant, attraction

COM or CON = *with, together;* also an intensifier (from Latin *cum*) (usually *con*, except before *m, p, b, r, l*)

com + m	commemorate, commercial, committee, commodity, communicate
com + p	compatible, compensate, competition, complicate, component
com + b	combat, combination, combustible
cor + r	correlate, correction, correspond, corrosion, corrupt
col + l	collaborate, collapse, collateral, collective, collision

DIS = *away, apart, deprive of, cause to be the opposite of*

dif + f	difference, difficulty, diffidence, diffuse

IN = *in, not;* also an intensifier

im + p	impartial, impetuous, impoverish, impractical, improvise
ir + r	irrational, irregular, irrelevant, irresistible, irrigate
il + l	illegal, illegible, illiterate, illuminate, illustration
im + m	immature, immigrant, immobile, immortal, immunity
im + b	imbalance, imbecile, imbibe, imbue

OB = *toward, for, about, before*

oc + c	occasion, occident, occult, occupation, occurrence
op + p	opponent, opportunity, opposite, oppression, opprobrium
of + f	offensive, offer, official

SUB = *under, below*

suc + c	successful, succinct, succumb, succor (help), successive
suf + f	suffer, suffice, sufficient, suffocate, suffrage
sug + g	suggestion, suggestive
sum + m	summarize, summit, summon
sup + p	supplement, suppliant, supplier, support, suppose, suppress

4. Word pairs often confused because of similarities in sound[10]

accept (verb)—receive willingly
    All the winners *accepted* their prizes in person.
except (preposition)—other than, but, excluding
    All the winners *except one* received their prizes in person.
adapt (verb)—adjust to new conditions
    She *adapts* herself very quickly to any new situation.
adopt (verb)—take as one's own
    The childless couple are trying to *adopt* a child.
advice (noun)—an opinion offered to help someone
    His lawyer has given him some good *advice.*
advise (verb)—give an opinion in order to help someone
    His doctor *advised* him to give up smoking.
beside (preposition)—next to, by the side of
    They placed an end table *beside* the armchair.
besides (preposition, adverb)—in addition (to)
    Besides his income, he gets a little money from an inheritance.
    I can't go to the movies with you because I have to study. *Besides,* I don't have any money.
complement (noun)—something that completes
    Most verbs have *complements.*
compliment (noun)—something said to praise or flatter
    He's very good at giving *compliments* to beautiful women.
conscience (noun)—an inner sense of what is right or wrong
    My *conscience* bothers me if I do something wrong.
conscious (adjective)—aware, in possession of one's senses
    The man was badly hurt but remained *conscious.*
désert (noun)—a dry sandy region
    The Sahara *Desert* is a vast expanse of dry, arid land.
desért (verb)—leave, abandon
    Her husband *deserted* her many years ago.
dessért (noun)—the final course of a meal, usually something sweet.
    We'll have some ice cream for *dessert.*

---

[10] Some of the words in this list may function as other parts of speech than those given here.

INDEX OF USAGE AND RHETORIC

effect (noun)—result
   Inflation will have a serious *effect* on the country's economy.

affect (verb)—influence, cause a change in
   Inflation will seriously *affect* the country's economy. (Note that *affect* = have an *effect* on.)

later (adverb)—after some time
   I can't see him now. He'll have to come back *later.*

latter (adjective)—near the end or close, the last mentioned of two
   The fire occurred in the *latter* part of January.
   She has a sister and a brother. The former lives in Florida, the *latter* in New York.

loose (adjective)—not tight
   She's gotten much thinner. Her clothes are now too *loose* on her.

lose (verb)—no longer have something
   Hold on to your ticket. You musn't *lose* it.

móral (noun)—lesson
   Each of Aesop's Fables has a *moral* about human behavior.

moréle (noun)—state of mind with respect to confidence, cheerfulness, discipline.
   After their defeat in battle, the *morale* of the Army was very low.

pérsonal (adjective)—private, individual
   They were able to rescue only a few *personal* belongings from the fire.

personnél (noun)—persons employed in a service or in a particular organization; the office where persons are hired
   If you are looking for a job, you must go to the *personnel* office.

principal (adjective)—chief
   Coffee is one of the *principal* products of Colombia.
   (noun)—chief person (in an elementary or high school)
   Her sister is the *principal* of a high school.
   (noun)—main amount of money
   He lost both *principal* and interest in a bad investment.

principle (noun)—rule, law
   He's studying the basic *principles* of physics.

quiet (adjective)—not noisy
   Late at night this street is very *quiet.*

quite (adverb)—very
   During the day this street is *quite* noisy.

stationary (adjective)—not movable
   This engine is *stationary*.
stationery (noun)—writing materials
   I'm going to the *stationery* store for some paper and envelopes.
than (conjunction used in comparison)
   He's taller *than* his brother.
then (adverb)—at that time, next in time
   First the soup is served, *then* the main dish.
their (adjective—possessive of *they*)
   They are very proud of *their* son.
they're (contraction of pronoun + verb)
   They're very proud of their son.
there (adverb)—in that place
   Put the packages over *there*.
weather (noun)—atmospheric conditions
   The *weather* is very cold today.
whether (conjunction introducing indirect yes–no questions)
   It doesn't matter *whether* we go or stay.
whose (adjective—possessive of *who*)
   Whose book is this?
who's (contraction of pronoun + verb)
   Who's coming to the party?
your (adjective—possessive of *you*)
   I believe this is *your* book.
you're (contraction of pronoun + verb)
   Thank you. *You're* welcome.

5. *160 frequently misspelled words*

1. abbreviate
2. absence
3. accidentally
4. accommodate
5. accompanying
6. accomplish
7. accumulate
8. achievement
9. acknowledge
10. acquaintance
11. acquire
12. acquitted
13. across
14. advertisement
15. amateur
16. analysis
17. analyze
18. apartment
19. apology
20. appearance
21. appropriate
22. arctic
23. argument
24. arrangement
25. association
26. attendance
27. audience
28. auxiliary
29. awkward
30. beginning

INDEX OF USAGE AND RHETORIC

31. benefited
32. boundaries
33. business
34. cafeteria
35. calendar
36. category
37. changeable
38. changing
39. characteristic
40. chosen
41. commission
42. committed
43. committee
44. comparative
45. comparison
46. competitive
47. compulsory
48. conceivable
49. conference
50. conqueror
51. conscientious
52. conscious
53. continuous
54. convenient
55. courteous
56. criticism
57. curiosity
58. decision
59. definitely
60. description
61. desperate
62. developed
63. disagree
64. disappoint
65. disastrous
66. discipline
67. dissatisfied
68. eighth
69. eligible
70. eliminate
71. embarrass
72. enthusiastic
73. environment
74. equipment
75. equivalent
76. especially
77. exaggerated
78. existence
79. experience
80. explanation
81. extremely
82. familiar
83. fascinate
84. February
85. generally
86. government
87. grammar
88. guidance
89. height
90. hindrance
91. humorous
92. hygiene
93. illiterate
94. immediately
95. incidentally
96. indefinitely
97. indispensable
98. inevitable
99. infinite
100. intellectual
101. irrelevant
102. irresistible
103. knowledge
104. laboratory
105. legitimate
106. lightning
107. loneliness
108. maintenance
109. maneuver
110. marriage
111. miniature
112. mischievous
113. ninety
114. noticeable
115. nowadays
116. obstacle
117. occasionally
118. occurrence
119. opportunity
120. outrageous
121. pamphlet
122. parallel
123. pastime
124. permissible
125. perseverance
126. physically
127. picnicking
128. precedence
129. preferred
130. prejudice
131. preparation
132. prevalent
133. privilege
134. probably
135. pronunciation
136. prove
137. recognize
138. reference
139. repetition
140. restaurant
141. rhythm
142. secretary
143. separate
144. similar
145. simultaneous
146. specifically
147. speech
148. surprise
149. symbolize
150. temperature
151. thorough
152. throughout
153. tragedy
154. truly
155. Tuesday
156. unanimous
157. unnecessarily
158. village
159. whether
160. writing

INDEX OF USAGE AND RHETORIC

trans

transition (between paragraphs)

The word *transition,* which means "go over" or "go across," refers to the smooth connection between paragraphs. There are two important means of establishing such connections between paragraphs.

1. *Lead-in transitions*

This kind of transition acts as a bridge between the general content of the introduction and the specific content of the main part of the composition. It may also suggest to the reader how the subject will be treated. Thus, in a composition about superstitions, after the introduction makes some general statements about superstitions, a lead-in sentence like: *My country has many superstitions about numbers, animals and birds, and things* can indicate to the reader that the composition will be organized in this order. The lead-in transition may be placed either at the end of the introductory paragraph or at the beginning of the next paragraph.

2. *Opening sentences of paragraphs*

As a transitional device, the opening sentence of a paragraph often: (a) makes clear the connection with the preceding paragraph; (b) introduces the new point from the outline; (c) includes a reference to the general subject of the composition. For example, in the composition about superstition, an opening sentence like: *My country also has many superstitions about things,* fulfills all three functions:

- **A.** *Also* is the connecting expression indicating that the information in the paragraph is being added to previously given types of superstition.
- **B.** *Things* suggests that this is the subject of the paragraph (from the point on the outline).
- **C.** *Superstitions* is repeated in this sentence to remind the reader of the general subject of the composition.

The following faults in transition should be avoided.

Faults in lead-in transitions

There is no transition at all between the general statements of the introduction and the first main point of the composition, with the result that there is a sharp break between these two parts of the composition. Or, if a transition is made, this transition is inadequate or unclear.

INDEX OF USAGE AND RHETORIC

Faults in opening sentences of paragraphs

A. The opening sentence of a paragraph does not make clear either the connection with the preceding paragraph or the subject of the new paragraph. Also, no reference is made to the general subject of the composition. The opening sentence must be a constant reminder to the reader of what the general subject of the composition is. For example, if the composition is about superstitions, the word *superstition* should appear in the opening sentence.

B. The opening sentence of a paragraph begins immediately with a detail, giving no indication of what the subject of the paragraph will be.

C. The transition used in the opening sentence of a paragraph is too repetitious of the preceding paragraph. Sometimes all that is needed for such a connection is a single word or a short phrase.

The following list gives some transitional expressions that can be used between paragraphs and also within paragraphs.

addition	moreover, in addition, furthermore, further, and, also, besides, likewise, as well as, too, not only ... but also, both ... and, another, still another
alternative	or, nor, either ... or, neither ... nor
cause	for, because, since, as, because of, on account of
comparison	*equal:* as ... as, the same as, similar to, like, alike, likewise, both, equally *unequal:* different from, unlike, dissimilar (for 2) ___-er than *or* more ___ than (for 3 or more) the ___-est *or* the most ___
condition	if, unless, provided that, in the event that, otherwise, or, if not, if so
contrast	however, still, nevertheless, anyway, instead, on the contrary, on the other hand, even so, but, yet, although, even though, while, whereas
example	for example, for instance, to illustrate, thus, as an illustration, e.g., such as, such ... as, like, in particular, particularly, specifically
introduction to a new point	as for, as to, with respect to, with reference to, with regard to, regarding, about, as far as ... is concerned

INDEX OF USAGE AND RHETORIC

manner	thus, in this way, in this manner, like, as, as if, as though
means	thus, thereby, by means of
place	here, there, beyond, opposite, facing, to the right, to the left, where(ver)
purpose	so that, (in order) to, in order that, for the purpose of, in the interest of
reinforcement of what has been said, or some degree of contradiction	in fact, as a matter of fact, actually, indeed, on the whole
repetition or restatement	in other words, that is to say, i.e.
result	so, therefore, consequently, hence, thus, accordingly, as a result, for this reason, that's why, so that, such (a) . . . that, so . . . that
sequence (order)	first,[11] second, third, etc.; in the first place, in the second place, etc.; then, after this, next, last, finally,[12] another, still another
summary, conclusion	to summarize, in short, briefly, to put it briefly, so much for ___, in conclusion, to conclude, to sum up, on the whole
time	meanwhile, henceforth, at the same time, eventually, at first, afterward(s), later, then, before, after, while, since, until, as, when
	contrasts for past and present time:
	past: then, formerly, in former times, previously, in the past, years ago
	present: now, at present, at the present time, in modern times, today, nowadays

vague

vague

A statement that is very general in relation to the point that is being made is considered vague. The statement should be rewritten so that the intended meaning is expressed exactly.

Words like *thing, aspect,* and *factor* have very broad meaning. They should not be used to substitute for words that have more specific meaning. Also, words like *nice,* and *interesting,* which convey only a general impression, should be avoided in favor of more exact words.

---

[11] The use of firstly, secondly, etc. is now considered somewhat old-fashioned.

[12] In the sense of *time, finally* and *at last* are synonyms meaning "after some time has passed": *Finally* (or *at last*) *they were able to get the apartment they wanted.* In a sequence, *finally* and *last* are synonyms: first . . . , second . . . , third . . . , *finally* (or *last*).

INDEX OF USAGE AND RHETORIC

UNACCEPTABLE: Education is another important *factor* needed for a democratic government.

CORRECTION: Education is another important *requirement* for a democratic government.

V

verb

The information about verbs is presented here under the following subdivisions:

1. Tense forms
   A. Chart of verb tenses
   B. Verb endings—*-s, -ing, -ed*
   C. Types of auxiliaries
2. Special notes on verb forms
   A. *Shall* or *will* for future time
   B. Active or passive voice
   C. Perfect tenses
   D. Progressive (continuous) forms of the tenses
   E. Verb forms in negatives and questions
3. Uses of the tenses
4. Special uses of the tense forms
   A. Use of the present tenses for future time
   B. Use of the past progressive tense
   C. Use of the progressive forms with *while*
   D. Use of the past perfect or past progressive tense with *just . . . when . . .*
   E. Imperative use of the verb
   F. Subjunctive use of the tense forms
   G. Use of past verb forms in sequence of tenses
   H. Use of the historical present tense
5. Agreement of the verb and the subject
6. Verbals (infinitives with *to*, participles with *-ing* or *-ed*)
   A. Forms of verbals
   B. Gerunds
   C. Verbs of physical perception
   D. Verbs followed by infinitives or *-ing* forms (gerunds)
7. Modal auxiliaries
   A. Forms of modal auxiliaries
   B. Meanings of modal auxiliaries
8. Irregular verbs

1. *Tense forms*

   A. Chart of verb tenses[13]

Tense	Active Voice		Passive Voice	
		Progressive (Continuous)		*Progressive (Continuous)*
Present	offer*, offers*	am / is / are } offering	am / is / are } offered	am / is / are } being offered
Past	offered*	was / were } offering	was / were } offered	was / were } being offered
Future	will / shall } offer	will / shall } be offering	will / shall } be offered	—
Present perfect	have / has } offered	have / has } been offering	have / has } been offered	—
Past perfect	had offered	had been offering	had been offered	—
Future perfect	will / shall } have offered	will / shall } have been offering	will / shall } have been offered	—

* These auxiliary-less verbs are called the *simple* present and the *simple* past.

[13] From Marcella Frank, *Modern English: Exercises for Non-native Speakers, Part 1, Parts of Speech* (Englewood Cliffs, N.J.: Prentice-Hall, 1972). Reprinted by permission.

INDEX OF USAGE AND RHETORIC

B. Verb endings: *-s, -ing, -ed*

(1) *-s* is added to a third person[14] singular verb.

>She love*s* to dance.

The only irregular forms for third person singular are *is, does, has*.

>*(See* **Spelling** for words like *teaches* and *tries* that add *-es.)*

(2) *-ing* is added for a progressive (continuous) verb.

>They are paint*ing* the house now.

(See **Spelling** for words like *stopping* and *changing* that add or drop a letter.)

(3) *-ed* is added for a regular verb:

>In the *past tense:*   They paint*ed* the house yesterday.
>In the *passive voice:*   The house was paint*ed* yesterday.
>In the *perfect tenses:*   They have paint*ed* the house recently.

(See **Spelling** for words like *stopped, changed,* and *agreed* that add or drop a letter.)

In the list of irregular verbs (**Verb, 8**) the second form of each verb is the *past tense* (*The people* **wore** *beautiful costumes at the carnival*). The third form is the past participle,[15] used for the *passive voice* (*Beautiful costumes* **were worn** *at the carnival*) and for the *perfect tenses* (*People* **have worn** *beautiful costumes at carnivals*).

---

[14] In grammar, the word *person* indicates the kind of subject that a verb has. First person subjects are *I, we;* second person subjects are *you.* All other subjects—the pronouns *he, she, it, they,* and all nouns—are third person.

[15] In this text, all past participles, whether regular or irregular, will be referred to as the *-ed* participle.

C. Types of auxiliaries[16]

Tense	**be**	+ **-ing** present participle for *progressive* forms	He *is opening* the door now.
	be	+ **-ed** past participle for *passive* forms	Many soldiers *were wounded* in the battle.
	have	+ **-ed** past participle for the *perfect* tenses	They *have* just *arrived*.
	shall–will	+ simple form of verb[17]	They *will arrive* soon.
Questions, negatives of auxiliary-less verbs	**do**	+ simple form of verb[17]	*Did* he *arrive* on time? He *didn't arrive* on time.
Modal	**can–could** **may–might** **should** **would** **must** **be able to** **ought to** **have to**	+ simple form of verb[17] These modal auxiliaries add a special meaning such as *ability, permission, possibility,* etc., to the meaning of the main part of the verb.	He *can* *should* } *speak* English. *must*

[16] From Marcella Frank, *Modern English: Exercises for Non-native Speakers, Part 1, Parts of Speech* (Englewood Cliffs, N.J.: Prentice-Hall, 1972). Reprinted by permission.

[17] The simple form of the verb is the infinitive without *to*, or the name of the verb.

Note that:

(1) After any form of the verb *be,* only two choices are possible: the *-ing* (present) participle for the *progressive* tense forms; the *-ed* (past) participle for the *passive* voice.

(2) After the auxiliary *have,* only the *-ed* participle is used.

When *have* is used as a second auxiliary, it never changes its form.

shall–should
will–would
can–could   *have* gone
must
ought to

2. Special notes on verb forms

A. Shall or will for future time

There is a rule that *shall* is used with *I* or *we* (first person) as subjects, and that *will* is used with all other subjects. However, in the United States, *will* is very common even with *I* and *we,* except in the most formal usage.

B. Active or passive voice

The same event may be referred to in either voice.

ACTIVE VOICE: Leon Tolstoy (subject) wrote *War and Peace* (object).
PASSIVE VOICE: *War and Peace* (original object) was written by Leon Tolstoy (original subject).

Note that in the passive voice:

(1) The verb consists of a form of *be* plus the *-ed* participle.

(2) The original subject becomes the object of the preposition *by.*

(3) The original object becomes the grammatical subject. For this reason, only transitive verbs (verbs that take an object) can be used in passive sentences.

The active voice, as a more direct statement of an action, is generally preferred. The passive voice is more appropriate when the "doer" of an action (or the agent) is unimportant or unknown, or when the speaker wishes to stress the "receiver" of the action. The passive voice is also preferred in formal writing that requires an impersonal tone.

INDEX OF USAGE AND RHETORIC

Sometimes, also, a passive verb is more desirable to allow the speaker to keep the same subject.

My dog ran out into the street and was hit by a car.

C. Perfect tenses

The term *perfect* means that a form of *have* is used as an auxiliary. Each of these three perfect tenses expresses a time that is *completed* in relation to another time.

Present perfect, completed in relation to present time (the moment of speaking):	We have studied ten chapters so far.
Past perfect, completed in relation to past time:	The prisoner who had escaped last week was captured yesterday.
Future perfect, completed in relation to future time:	By December, all the leaves will have fallen from the trees.

D. Progressive (continuous) forms of the tenses

The progressive forms usually emphasize the *duration* of an event, that is, the event lasts or continues. These forms are used mainly with verbs of *action*.

In the present tense, the progressive form is the real present; the simple form is used mostly for "timeless" situations (see **Verb, 3**). In the other tenses, however, the progressive forms often represent alternate ways of expressing the same time event, the difference being the *emphasis on the duration*.

Past progressive:	They were making a lot of noise at the party last night.
Present perfect progressive:	Since his graduation from college, he has been working in his father's company.
Past perfect progressive:	The children had been fighting for some time before their mother stopped them.
Future perfect progressive:	By the time you get there, they will have been rehearsing for several hours.

The future progressive form is more likely to imply closeness to the present than duration of an event.

The plane will be leaving soon.

(See **Verb, 4,** for special uses of the progressive forms.)

INDEX OF USAGE AND RHETORIC

E. Verb forms in negatives and questions

Auxiliaries play a role in the production of negatives and questions.

SENTENCE: The plane *has* arrived.
NEGATIVE: The plane *has not* (or *hasn't*) arrived. (*Not* is added after the auxiliary for a negative.)
QUESTION: *Has* the plane arrived? (The auxiliary and the subject are reversed in a question.)[18]

If the verb has no auxiliary (simple present and simple past tenses), the auxiliary *do* is added.

SENTENCE: The plane arrived.
NEGATIVE: The plane *did not* (or *didn't*) arrive.
QUESTION: *Did* the plane arrive?

However, if a form of the independent verb *be* has no auxiliary, this form functions in the same way as auxiliaries do in negatives and questions.

SENTENCE: He *is* nervous today.
NEGATIVE: He *is not* (or *isn't*) nervous today.
QUESTION: *Is* he nervous today?

---

[18] The one exception to this reversal of auxiliary and subject occurs when a question word is the subject: *What has arrived?*

3. *Uses of the tenses*

Tense	Kind of Time	Possible Time Expressions	Comments, Examples
Simple present	1. "timeless" —includes present, past, future time		
	involves *repetition*: general statements	frequency words: always, sometimes, often, usually, twice, etc.	*He always comes to work on time.*
			The earth revolves around the sun.
	customary actions or events		*Americans celebrate Thanksgiving on the last Thursday in November.*
	2. present state or condition, with nonaction verbs like *love, remember, need*		*I need more paper to finish typing this report.*
			I remember how beautiful this city once was.
Present progressive	true present time	now, today, at present	
	1. expresses a *single action* (that has a possible beginning, middle, and end)		*The repairman is fixing the TV set now.*
	2. may express the beginning, middle, or end of an action		*They are beginning to work on the new bridge today.*
			(continued)

3. Uses of the tenses (cont.)

Tense	Kind of Time	Possible Time Expressions	Comments, Examples
Past	time that *definitely* finished in the past	yesterday, last year, a week ago, in the past, once	*In the past, the chief means of transportation was a horse and carriage.*
Future	time that will occur after the present time	tomorrow, in a week, next year, in the future	*We will finish the work tomorrow.*
Present perfect	past to present time indefinite time in the past	for, since frequency words: often, seldom, once, etc.	*He has lived in London for forty years.* (He is still living there.) but: *He lived in London for forty years.* (He is no longer living there, or he is no longer alive.)
	time ends at the moment of speaking	so far, up to now	Informally, except with *since* and *for*, the past tense often replaces the present perfect tense.
	may be recent past	recently, lately	
Past perfect	past time before another past time		Used in narration: *The burglar alarm went off and a crowd began to gather. Soon the police arrived at the scene of the robbery. But they were too late. The thieves had already gone.*

			Used in an adverbial clause, especially time: *After I had spoken, I realized my mistake.*
			Used in an adjective clause: *The man who had stolen the money two weeks ago confessed last night.*
			Informally, except for the first example, the past tense often replaces the past perfect tense in such sentences.
Future perfect	future time which ends *at*, *before*, or *by* another future time	on, when, at	*When he retires, he will have made more than a million dollars.*
	the future perfect time often begins in the past	by *(most common)*	*By the end of the school year, we will have covered the entire grammar book.*
		before	*Before his vacation is over, he will have made many new friends.*

INDEX OF USAGE AND RHETORIC

4. *Special uses of the tense forms*

    A. **Use of the present tenses for future time**

    (1) With an expression of future time accompanying the verb:

Simple present, with verbs of arriving and departing, especially for traveling:	The plane leaves in an hour.
Present progressive: with most verbs expressing action:	They are giving a party tomorrow.
Be going to, with all verbs (the expression of future time may be omitted):	Our house is going to be painted next week.

    (2) In time clauses and conditional clauses, with or without an expression of future time:

    TIME: After he *graduates* from college, he will take a vacation in Europe.
    CONDITION: If I *finish* my work early enough, I'll go to the movies with you.

    B. **Use of the past progressive tense**

   The past progressive tense is used to indicate a past action in progress that is interrupted by another past action.

         We were eating dinner when we heard a loud noise outside.
   OR: While we were eating dinner, we heard a loud noise outside.

   In both choices, the act of eating dinner is in progress when it is interrupted by the noise outside.

    C. **Use of the progressive forms with *while***

   Progressive forms are used for two actions that are in progress at the same time. These progressive forms are optional; they may occur with one or both of the actions.

   While she *was doing* (or *did*) her homework, her brother *was watching* (or *watched*) television.

    D. **Use of the past perfect or past progressive tense with *just . . . when . . .***

If a *when* clause follows a verb with *just, already, scarcely,* or *barely,* the past perfect tense is required to express an action that comes before another one.

The guests had *just* (or *already*) finished dessert when a late dinner guest arrived.

With *just* and *already,* a past progressive verb is used if the action is in progress when it is interrupted by another past action.

The guests were *just* (or *already*) having dessert when a late dinner guest arrived. (This sentence is similar to the first example under B above.)

E. Imperative use of the verb

The imperative form of the verb (the infinitive without *to*) is used for requests, commands, and suggestions.

POSITIVE: Please *open* the package.
NEGATIVE: Please *don't open* the package.

When the imperative is used with *let's,* the suggestion includes the speaker and the person addressed.

POSITIVE: Let's *open* the package.
NEGATIVE: Let's *not open* the package.

F. Subjunctive use of the tense forms

(1) Past tense for present time

Unreal conditions:	If I were[19] at home now, I would be watching television.
Wishes (after the verb *wish* only):	I wish I were at home now.
Conjecture (after verbs like *act as if, look as if,* if the speaker is not certain about the statement):	He looks as if (or as though) he *needed* more sleep. (But, *needs* if the speaker is more certain about his or her impression.)

(2) Past perfect tense for past time

Unreal conditions:	If I had been at home yesterday, I would have been watching television.

---

[19] For the verb *be*, only *were* is appropriate in formal English. However, *was* is often heard informally.

INDEX OF USAGE AND RHETORIC

Wishes (after the verb *wish* only): I wish I had been at home yesterday.

Conjecture: The man acts as though he had been spoiled when he was a child.

(3) Simple form of the verb for present, past, or future time

The simple form of the verb (the infinitive without *to*) occurs:

After verbs like *suggest, recommend, command, advise, demand, urge, ask*

The doctor recommended (*or* recommends, will recommend, has recommended) that his patient *take* a long rest from his work.

After adjectives like *important, necessary, required*

It is important that the patient *take* a long rest.

In such sentences the auxiliary *should* often occurs with the simple form of the verb.

The doctor recommended that his patient *should take* a long rest from his work.

However, *should* is not used after strong verbs like *demand, command*.

G. Use of past verb forms in sequence of tenses

If the main verb of a sentence is past, the other verbs in the sentence usually have past form also, especially in formal English.

Present Main Verb	**Past Main Verb**
He *says* that he *has* a headache.	He *said* that he *had* a headache.
He *tells* me he *is* planning to retire.	He *told* me he *was* planning to retire.
Although they *want* to move, they *can't* find another apartment.	Although they *wanted* to move, they *couldn't* find another apartment.

H. Use of the historical present tense

In a story or a summary, the present tense may be used instead of the past tense to create a more vivid and dramatic effect.

After her sisters leave for the ball, Cinderella sits near the fire and weeps. The French philosopher Descartes claims that he exists because he thinks.

In using this historical present tense, the student should be careful not to change to the past tense. The same tense must be continued throughout the story or the summary.

5. *Agreement of the verb and the subject*

English grammar requires that the verb agree in number with the main word of the subject. Such agreement is especially important with subjects that are in the *third person singular.* Actually, this agreement is needed mainly:

With verbs in the simple present

      That girl *talks* a lot. (third person singular subject)
BUT: Those girls *talk* a lot. (third person plural subject)

With forms of *be, have,* and *do* as auxiliaries

be: *present* The girl *is* watching television.
        BUT: The girls *are* watching TV.

    past   The girl *was* watching television.
        BUT: The girls *were* watching TV.

have: The girl *has* finished her work.
  BUT: The girls *have* finished their work.

do: The girl *does* not like to work.
  BUT: The girls *do* not like to work.

In verbs with more than one auxiliary, the agreement occurs *only with the first auxiliary.*

(Refer to **Agreement** for more information about the agreement between subject and verb.)

6. *Verbals (infinitives with* to, *participles with* -ing *or* -ed)

    A. Forms of verbals

Infinitive					
to open	to be	{ opening opened	to have opened	to have been	{ opening opened
Participle					
opening opened	being opened		having opened	having been	{ opening opened

INDEX OF USAGE AND RHETORIC

Verbals without the auxiliary *have* are "timeless." The time they refer to is suggested by the time of the main verb.

> It is beginning *to rain.* (*To rain* represents present time.)
> It began *to rain.* (*To rain* represents past time.)

Verbals with the auxiliary *have* (perfect forms) refer to time that precedes the time of the main verb.

> It's better to have loved and lost than never to have loved at all. (The *loving and losing* are in the past.)
> vs: It's better to love and lose than never to love at all. (*Loving and losing* correspond to the "timeless" present tense.)

As in the use of the past perfect tense, the perfect form of a verbal is preferred if the speaker wishes to *emphasize* that one action happened before the other.

> He admitted having stolen the money. (Emphasis is on the fact that the stealing of the money occurred before he admitted the theft.)
> vs: He admitted stealing the money. (The speaker does not wish to mark a careful sequencing of actions in the past.)

B. Gerunds

Verbals often function as nouns, that is, as subjects or objects. The *-ing* participial form used as a noun is called a *gerund*.

> GERUND: *Seeing* is *believing.*

Only the *-ing* form of the verb is used after prepositions.

> On *hearing* the news, she began to cry.
> After *typing* the letter, the secretary handed it to her boss for his signature.

C. Verbs of physical perception

Verbs of physical perception may be followed by either the *to*-less infinitive (*watch someone **do** something*) or the *-ing* participle (*watch someone **doing** something*). These verbs are: *feel, hear, listen to, notice, observe, perceive, see, watch, witness.*

INDEX OF USAGE AND RHETORIC

D. Verbs followed by infinitives or *-ing* forms (gerunds)

Verbs + *-ing* Forms
(*admit **doing** something*)

admit	finish	quit (= stop, *informal*)
anticipate	give up	recommend
appreciate	imagine	regret (*for the past*)[20]
avoid	keep (on)	remember (*for the past*)[21]
consider (= keep in mind)	miss	resent
delay	postpone	resist
deny	practice	risk
enjoy	put off	stop
		suggest

Verbs + either the Infinitive or the *-ing* Forms
(*attempt **to do** or **doing** something*)

attempt	like
begin	love
continue	neglect
dislike	plan
hate	prefer
hesitate	start
intend	

Verbs + Infinitives
(*afford **to do** something*)

afford	hope
arrange	learn
consent	manage
decide	pretend
deserve	refuse
determine	swear
endeavor	threaten
forget	volunteer

---

[20] *Regret* is followed by the infinitive when it does not refer to past time: *We regret to inform you that the trip has been canceled.*

[21] *Remember* is followed by the infinitive when it means "remind oneself about something in the future": *We must remember to buy tickets for the ballet as soon as we arrive in town.*

INDEX OF USAGE AND RHETORIC

Verbs + Objects + Infinitives
(*advise* **someone to do** *something*)

advise	encourage	request
allow	expect[22]	require
beg[22]	forbid	teach
cause	force	tell
challenge	instruct	urge
command	invite	want[22]
convince	order	warn
dare (= challenge)	permit	wish[22]
desire[22]	persuade	would like[22]
enable	remind	

Verbs + *to*-less Infinitives
(*make* **someone do** *something*)

make
have
help[23]
let

7. Modal auxiliaries

A. Forms of modal auxiliaries

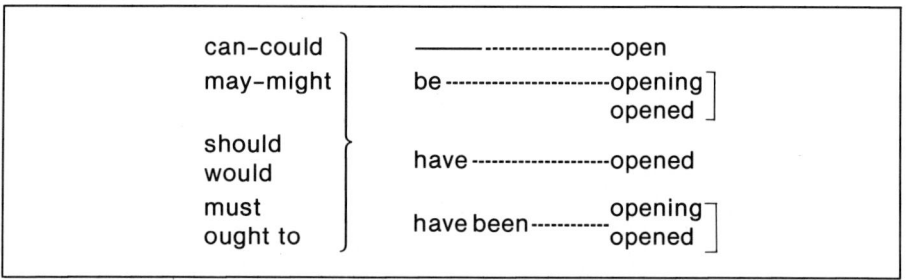

Those modals with *be* as the second auxiliary are the progressive or passive forms.

PROGRESSIVE: She's not at her desk; she *may be taking* her afternoon break.
PASSIVE: Their financial problems *could be solved* if they had more efficient management.

---

[22] These verbs can also be used without an object before the infinitive (*expect **to do** something*).
[23] *Help* can also be followed by the infinitive with *to* (*help someone **to do** something*).

The modals with *have* or *have been* usually express past time.

have: The streets are wet; it *must have rained* last night.

have been:

    PROGRESSIVE: He *should have been saving* for the future instead of spending all his money.
    PASSIVE: The accident *could have been prevented* if he had been more careful.

You will note that *be* or *have* as the second auxiliary after a modal never changes its form.

B. Meanings of modal auxiliaries

Ability—can, be able to

    PHYSICAL ABILITY: I can (*or* am able to) move this table by myself.
    LEARNED ABILITY: She can (*or* is able to) type 80 words a minute.

Permission—may, can

May (*or* can) I borrow your car tonight?

Could is also used in asking for permission.

Could I borrow your car tonight?

Obligation, advisability—should, ought to, had better

You should (*or* ought to, had better) study for that test.
You should (*or* ought to) have studied for yesterday's test. (The form with *have* implies that the action was not performed.)

Necessity—must, have to, need to

Everyone must (*or* has to) obey the law.

In some sentences, *must, have to* may be stronger alternatives for *should, ought to*.

Everyone *should* obey the law.

In other sentences such choices are not possible.

Everyone *must* eat in order to survive.

Expectation—should, ought to

They left at five o'clock.
  They should be here soon. (present or future time)
  They should have arrived long ago. (past time)

INDEX OF USAGE AND RHETORIC

Possibility—may-might, can-could

> It may (*or* might) rain tonight.
> Something can (*or* could) go wrong with our plans.

The past forms *might* or *could* express less certainty.

> For actual past time, *may have, might have,* or *could have* are used for possibility.

> I can't find my wallet. I *might have left* it at home.

Inference—must

> Nobody's in the office.
>   They must be out to lunch. (present time)
>   They must have left for lunch. (past time)

Instructions—should, must

> You should (*or stronger,* must) wash the floor before you wax it.

These forms are alternatives for the imperative.

> Wash the floor before you wax it.

Recommendation—should, must

> This wine is excellent. You should (*or stronger,* must) try it.

Past custom—used to, would

> When I was young, I used to (*or* would) play tennis very often. (but now I don't)

Present custom requires *be used to.*

> I am used to playing tennis every morning before I go to work. (Here *used to* is a synonym for *accustomed to.*)

Preference—would rather

> I would rather stay at home than go to the movies. (preference about present or "timeless" time)
> I would rather have stayed at home than (have) gone to the movies. (preference about past time)

Note that the verbs after *than* (*go, have gone*) have the same grammatical form as the verbs after *would rather.*

8. *Irregular verbs*[24]

Simple Form of the Verb	Past Tense	Past Participle
arise	arose	arisen
awake	awoke (*sometimes* awaked)	awaked (*Brit.* awoke, awoken)
be	was	been
bear	bore	borne (*meaning* carry)
		born (*meaning* have children)
beat	beat	beaten (*sometimes* beat)
become	became	become
begin	began	begun
bend	bent	bent
bet	bet (*sometimes* betted)	bet (*sometimes* betted)
bid (*meaning* offer money at an auction)	bid	bid
bid (*meaning* ask someone to do something)	bade (*or* bid)	bidden (*or* bid)
bind	bound	bound
bite	bit	bitten (*or* bit)
bleed	bled	bled
blow	blew	blown
break	broke	broken
breed	bred	bred
bring	brought	brought
broadcast	broadcast (*sometimes* broadcasted)	broadcast (*sometimes* broadcasted)
build	built	built
burst	burst	burst
buy	bought	bought
cast	cast	cast
catch	caught	caught
choose	chose	chosen
cling	clung	clung
come	came	come

[24] Revised from Marcella Frank, *Modern English: Exercises for Non-native Speakers, Part 1, Parts of Speech* (Englewood Cliffs, N.J.: Prentice-Hall, 1972), pp. 205–8. Reprinted by permission.

INDEX OF USAGE AND RHETORIC

Simple Form of the Verb	Past Tense	Past Participle
cost	cost	cost
creep	crept	crept
dig	dug	dug
dive	dived (*or* dove)	dived
do	did	done
draw	drew	drawn
dream	dreamt (*more often* dreamed)	dreamt (*more often* dreamed)
drink	drank	drunk
drive	drove	driven
eat	ate	eaten
fall	fell	fallen
feed	fed	fed
feel	felt	felt
fight	fought	fought
find	found	found
flee	fled	fled
fling	flung	flung
fly	flew	flown
forbid	forbade (*or* forbad)	forbidden
forget	forgot	forgotten (*Brit.* forgot)
forsake	forsook	forsaken
freeze	froze	frozen
get	got	gotten (*Brit.* got)
give	gave	given
go	went	gone
grind	ground	ground
grow	grew	grown
hang	hung / hanged (*meaning suspended by the neck*)	hung / hanged (*meaning suspended by the neck*)
have	had	had
hear	heard	heard
hide	hid	hidden (*or* hid)
hit	hit	hit
hold	held	held
hurt	hurt	hurt
keep	kept	kept
kneel	knelt (*or* kneeled)	knelt (*or* kneeled)
knit	knit (*or* knitted)	knit (*or* knitted)
know	knew	known
lay	laid	laid
lead	led	led
leap	lept (*more often* leaped)	lept (*more often* leaped)

INDEX OF USAGE AND RHETORIC

Simple Form of the Verb	Past Tense	Past Participle
leave	left	left
lend	lent	lent
let	let	let
lie	lay	lain
light	lit (*more often* lighted)	lit (*more often* lighted)
lose	lost	lost
make	made	made
mean	meant	meant
meet	met	met
mislay	mislaid	mislaid
mistake	mistook	mistaken
overcome	overcame	overcome
pay	paid	paid
put	put	put
read	read	read
rid	rid	rid
ride	rode	ridden
ring	rang	rung
rise	rose	risen
run	ran	run
say	said	said
see	saw	seen
seek	sought	sought
sell	sold	sold
send	sent	sent
set	set	set
sew	sewed	sewn (*or* sewed)
shake	shook	shaken
shed	shed	shed
shine (*intrans.*)	shone	shone
shoot	shot	shot
show	showed	shown (*or* showed)
shrink	shrank (*also* shrunk)	shrunk
shut	shut	shut
sing	sang	sung
sink	sank (*also* sunk)	sunk
sit	sat	sat
sleep	slept	slept
slide	slid	slid
slit	slit	slit
speak	spoke	spoken
speed	sped (*or* speeded)	sped (*or* speeded)
spend	spent	spent
spin	spun	spun
spit	spit (*sometimes* spat)	spit (*sometimes* spat)

INDEX OF USAGE AND RHETORIC

Simple Form of the Verb	Past Tense	Past Participle
split	split	split
spread	spread	spread
spring	sprang (*also* sprung)	sprung
stand	stood	stood
steal	stole	stolen
stick	stuck	stuck
sting	stung	stung
stink	stank (*also* stunk)	stunk
stride	strode	stridden
strike	struck	struck
string	strung	strung
strive	strove (*also* strived)	striven (*also* strived)
swear	swore	sworn
sweep	swept	swept
swim	swam	swum
swing	swung	swung
take	took	taken
teach	taught	taught
tear	tore	torn
tell	told	told
think	thought	thought
thrive	throve (*or* thrived)	thriven (*or* thrived)
throw	threw	thrown
thrust	thrust	thrust
undergo	underwent	undergone
understand	understood	understood
wake	woke (*sometimes* waked)	waked (*Brit.* woke, woken)
wear	wore	worn
weave	wove	woven
weep	wept	wept
win	won	won
wind	wound	wound
withdraw	withdrew	withdrawn
withhold	withheld	withheld
withstand	withstood	withstood
wring	wrung	wrung
write	wrote	written

WF

word form

Nouns, adjectives, verbs, and adverbs often have characteristic endings (suffixes). An awareness of the physical signals for these parts of speech will

INDEX OF USAGE AND RHETORIC

make it easier for students to know which part-of-speech form to use. The signals that identify a part of speech are its function, its position, its form, and its "markers" (special words that precede it).

The following chart gives common word forms for nouns, adjectives, verbs, and adverbs, as well as the function, position, and markers that identify each of these parts of speech.

Forms and Markers	Function	Position	Example
Nouns			
-ment, -tion, -ing, -hood, -ship, -ence, -ness, -er, -age, etc.	subject	before the verb	The *examination* was very difficult.
	object of the verb	after the verb	She dislikes *arguments*.
Markers (precede nouns): determiners	object of the preposition	after the preposition	He became more serious after his *marriage*.
articles—*a, the* demonstratives—*this, that* possessives—*my, John's*, etc. words of indefinite quantity—*some, many*, etc. numbers—*one, the first*, etc.	(subjective) complement appositive	after a linking verb (mostly *be*) after another noun	He is a good *administrator*. Mr. Johnson, the famous *actor*, will play the leading role.
Adjectives			
-less, -ful, -ous, -ish, -ent, -ible, -ing, -ed, etc.	modifier of a noun or pronoun	before the noun	*Careless* drivers can cause accidents.
Markers (precede adjectives): words showing "how much" (degree)—*very, quite, extremely*, etc.		after a linking verb (*be, seem, appear, look, become*, etc.)	He's very *sensible*.

83

INDEX OF USAGE AND RHETORIC

Forms and Markers	Function	Position	Example
Verbs *-ize, -fy, -en,* etc.	The grammatical center of the sentence	after the subject	The foundation of the building *has weakened.*
Markers (precede the main part of the verb—they are also part of the verb): auxiliaries—*have, can,* etc.		before the object	The police *have intensified* their search for the killer.
Adverbs mostly *-ly* added to adjectives also *-ward, -wise, -where*	modifier of a verb, an adjective, another adverb, or the whole sentence	initial	He scolded his secretary: *afterward* he was sorry.
		mid (with the verb)	They *frequently* go to the movies.
Markers (precede adverbs): the same as for adjectives		final	We can see poverty *everywhere.*

It may be necessary to check the dictionary to find the appropriate ending for a word used as a particular part of speech. If you wish to check further on the signals in a sentence that indicate which part of speech is required, consult the unit on Parts of Speech in the Grammar Review and Practice section.

WO

word order

∽ reverse the word order

The following rules about the correct word order should be observed.

1. In a question, *the order of the subject and the auxiliary is reversed.*

    STATEMENT: The play will begin now.
    QUESTION: Will the play begin soon?
    OR: When will the play begin?

INDEX OF USAGE AND RHETORIC

(See **Verb, 2E,** for more information about subject-auxiliary reversal in questions.)

2. In indirect questions, *no change is made from the normal subject–verb order.*

    QUESTION: Did the train arrive on time?
    INDIRECT
    QUESTION: He asked whether *the train had arrived* on time.

    QUESTION: When will the train arrive?
    INDIRECT
    QUESTION: He asked when *the train would arrive.*

However, if the question has the following form:

    who or **what**   + a form of the   + a noun or a pro-
                           independent verb *be*   noun

the verb appears at *the end of an indirect question.*

    QUESTION: What is her name?
    INDIRECT
    QUESTION: He asked what her name *was.*

    QUESTION: Who are they?
    INDIRECT
    QUESTION: He asked who they *were.*

3. Certain expressions used at the beginning of a sentence for emphasis require a reversal of subject and auxiliary.

    A. negatives or near negatives

    At no time should this door be left unlocked.
    Never have we seen such a terrible sight.
    Not only did he pass the examination, but he received an excellent grade.

    B. *only, so*

    Only after he lost her did he realize how much he loved her.
    So extensive was the damage that the house had to be completely rebuilt.

    C. expressions of place (especially with the independent verb *be*)

    In the room were some very distinguished visitors.

4. Adverbs and adverbial expressions have three possible positions in a sentence or clause.

    INITIAL POSITION: *Sometimes* he spends too much money.
    MID-POSITION
    (with the verb):   He *sometimes* spends too much money.
                          He has *sometimes* spent too much money.
    FINAL POSITION: He spends too much money *sometimes.*

An adverbial is usually not placed between a verb and its object.

> UNACCEPTABLE: He speaks *very well* English.
> CORRECTION: He speaks English *very well*.

Not all adverbs or adverbial expressions can be used in all positions, and in some sentences one position is more common than another. For example, adverbs of manner (such as *quietly, politely,* and *gracefully*) usually appear in midposition or final position.

> The thief *quickly* removed the contents of the safe.
> The thief removed the contents of the safe *quickly*.

Adverbs of manner in initial position are used mainly for emphasis.

> *Quickly,* the thief removed the contents of the safe.

For short single-word adverbs of frequency (such as *often, rarely,* and *always*) midposition is more common. *Never, seldom,* and *always* are rarely found in initial or final position. (See **3.A** for negatives and near negatives in initial position.)

Sentence adverbs (such as *clearly* and *obviously*) and conjunctive adverbs (such as *therefore* and *however*) are most likely to appear in initial or midposition.

> *Fortunately,* the rain didn't begin until they got home.
> The rain, *fortunately,* didn't begin until they got home.

These adverbs occur in final position only if the sentence is short.

> They got home before the rain, *fortunately.*

Adverbials of definite time (such as *yesterday, today,* and *tomorrow*) appear more often in final position, but they are also found in initial position.

> They delivered some of the furniture *yesterday.*
> *Tomorrow* they will deliver the rest.

If several adverbials are used after a verb, the usual order is *place, manner, time.*

> The soldiers marched through the town (place) quickly (manner) during the night (time).

Actually, the order of adverbials in final position is somewhat flexible, but adverbials of time usually remain last.

> The soldiers marched quickly (manner) through the town (place) during the night (time).

Adverbials should be placed in a position that clearly indicates the part of the sentence they refer to.

INDEX OF USAGE AND RHETORIC

AMBIGUOUS: A man who lies *frequently* will cheat also.
CORRECTION: A man who *frequently* lies will cheat also.
OR: A man who lies will *frequently* cheat also.

In formal English, adverbs like *only, just,* and *hardly* should be placed directly before the words they refer to.

INFORMAL: He *even* works during his vacation.
FORMAL: He works *even* during his vacation.

5. Adjectives have two usual positions.

BEFORE THE NOUN: A *beautiful* girl attracts a lot of attention.
AFTER A VERB
LIKE *BE* (linking verb): The girl is *beautiful.*

(See Parts of Speech in the Grammar Review and Practice section, identifying characteristics of adjectives, for more information about the position of adjectives.)

If more than one adjective is used before a noun, the following order is observed.

Words like *a, the, many, some, several* (determiners)	Numerals	General descriptive adjectives	Adjectives of physical description	Proper adjectives of nationality, religion, etc.	Other nouns	Nouns
the	**two**	**brilliant**	**young**	**American**	**folk**	**singers**

6. An indirect object precedes the direct object.

He gave his wife (indirect object) some flowers (direct object).

The indirect object may also appear after the direct object in a *to* phrase.

He gave some flowers (direct object) to his wife (indirect object).

(See Understanding Sentences, Exercise 2, in the Grammar Review and Practice section, for verbs that can take two objects.)

Some verbs use only the *to* phrase for the indirect object. This phrase must be placed *after the direct object.*

UNACCEPTABLE: He introduced to us his proposal.
CORRECTION: He introduced his proposal to us.

UNACCEPTABLE: Can you suggest me a good book?
CORRECTION: Can you suggest a good book to me?

Other common verbs like *introduce* and *suggest* in the above example are *describe, explain, recommend.*

INDEX OF USAGE AND RHETORIC

7. In an exclamation, normal subject-verb order is used after the exclamatory phrase.

    UNACCEPTABLE: How beautiful was the bride!
    CORRECTION: How beautiful the bride was!

(See Understanding Sentences, Exercise 4, in the Grammar Review and Practice section for the construction of exclamations.)

8. Idioms consisting of two parts—a verb and a preposition—may often be separated so that the object can appear between the two parts.

    TWO PARTS
    NOT SEPARATED: I must look up this word.
    TWO PARTS
    SEPARATED: I must look this word up.

If a pronoun object is used, the pronoun may be placed only between the two parts.

    I must look it up.

It is important to know which verbs are separable so that the right word order will be used with pronoun objects. The following is a list of the most common separable verbs.

    back up—cause to move backwards; support
    blow up—cause to explode
    break down—analyze, classify
    break in—begin to use
    break in(to)—enter a place forcibly
    break off—end suddenly
    break up—separate or scatter
    bring about—cause to happen
    bring on—cause
    bring out—emphasize, publish
    bring up—raise from childhood; raise a subject
    call off—cancel (a scheduled event)
    call up—telephone
    carry out—fulfill, perform
    clear up—clarify
    close down—close permanently
    cross off *or* out—eliminate (from writing)
    cut out—eliminate
    do over—do again
    figure out—interpret, understand
    fill in *or* out—complete (a printed form)
    fill up—fill completely (a container)
    find out—discover
    give away—give (as a gift)

INDEX OF USAGE AND RHETORIC

give back—return (something)
give out—distribute
give up—surrender (something)
hand down—leave as an inheritance
hand in—submit
hand out—distribute
hold up—rob, by threatening force
keep up—continue
leave out—omit
let down—disappoint
look over—examine
look up—search for information in a reference work
make out—see or understand with difficulty
make up—invent; apply cosmetics
mix up—confuse
pass out—distribute
pick out—select
pick up—lift; come to get (someone or something)
point out—indicate
put off—postpone
put on—dress in
put out—extinguish
set up—arrange
take off—remove (clothes); take leave (from work)
take over—assume command of
think over—consider
throw away—discard (because not needed)
try on—put on (a garment) to see how it fits and looks
try out—test
turn down—reject; lower the volume (of a radio, etc.)
turn in—submit
turn off—stop the operation of (a machine, etc.)
turn on—start the operation of (a machine, etc.)
wear out—use something until no longer usable; tire greatly
write down—record
write out—spell out
write up—prepare (a report, or similar document)

wordy

wordy

In this kind of fault, too many words have been used to express a particular idea.

> WORDY: In order to get a good education, people have to realize that it is not enough to specialize in only one field. A journalist who knows some history and a few languages can do a bet-

INDEX OF USAGE AND RHETORIC

> ter job in his field than let's say a journalist who does not have a clear conception of history. This example proves that other fields help increase the person's education to a considerable degree.
>
> IMPROVED: To get a good education, a person must specialize in more than one field. A journalist who knows some history and a few languages can do a better job than one who does not.

Certain expressions may also be unnecessary for the idea being expressed. For example, the words in parentheses can be omitted from the following: *green (in color), large (in size), in (the months of) July and August.*

WW

wrong word

Choose the exact word to express what you want to say. If necessary, refer to a dictionary or a thesaurus (a dictionary of synonyms).

Following are some word pairs that may be confused.

bring up (verb—transitive)[25]—raise (children)
>They *are bringing up* their children to respect other people.

grow up (verb—intransitive)—mature, become an adult
>Their children *grew up* in a good family atmosphere.

call off (verb—transitive)—cancel
>The picnic *was called off* because of rain.

put off (verb—transitive)—postpone
>Don't *put off* for tomorrow what you can do today.

lay (verb—transitive)—put, place
>He *laid* the book on the table.

lie (verb—intransitive)—rest, recline
>The book *is lying* on the desk.

raise (verb—transitive)—lift, cause to move upward
>Please *raise* the window a little. It's hot in here.

rise (verb—intransitive)—get up, stand up, move upward
>Prices *have been rising* very rapidly.

---

[25] A transitive verb takes an object; an intransitive verb does not.

INDEX OF USAGE AND RHETORIC

aspect (noun)—view, side
    The committee is investigating every *aspect* of the problem.

respect (noun)—a particular point or detail
    The committee found the report correct in every *respect*.

Certain connecting words are sometimes used incorrectly.

during used for *while*

UNACCEPTABLE:	*During* he was watching television, he fell asleep. (*During* is a preposition and can be followed only by a noun.)
CORRECTION:	*While* he was watching television, he fell asleep. (*While* is a conjunction that permits a subject and a predicate to follow it.)
OR:	*During* the television program he fell asleep. (*During* introduces the noun *program*.)

even used for *even if*

UNACCEPTABLE:	Students who are nervous during tests, *even* they are intelligent and well prepared, may not do well on the tests.
CORRECTION:	Students who are nervous during tests, *even if* they are intelligent and well prepared, may not do well on the tests.

after used for *after this, then,* or *next*

UNACCEPTABLE:	Let the water boil. *After* put in the rice.
CORRECTION:	Let the water boil. *After this* (or *then, next*) put in the rice.

no matter used for *no matter whether*

UNACCEPTABLE:	*No matter* we mean present or past time, we do not make a change in the verb.
CORRECTION:	*No matter whether* we mean present or past time, we do not make a change in the verb.

even though used for *even so*

UNACCEPTABLE:	Maybe she did hurt his feelings. *Even though* he shouldn't have hit her.
CORRECTION:	Maybe she did hurt his feelings. *Even so* he shouldn't have hit her. (*Even so* is an informal equivalent of *however*.)

Grammar Review and Practice

UNIT 1   Understanding Sentences   *94*
UNIT 2   Parts of Speech   *100*
UNIT 3   Complex Structures   *110*

UNIT ONE
Understanding Sentences

Most sentences contain two parts:

1. *The subject:* *who* or *what* the speaker is talking about.
2. *The predicate:* what the speaker is saying about the subject.

For example, in the sentence *John kissed Mary:*

John is the subject. It is the topic of discussion.

kissed Mary is the predicate. It is what is being said about the subject (actually, the predicate is everything that is not in the subject).

The predicate usually has two main elements:

1. *The verb:* the element that expresses what is happening. In this sentence, it is *kissed.*
2. *The complement:* the essential element that completes the statement made by the subject and the verb. In this sentence it is *Mary.*

You will note that the subject usually appears *before the verb,* the complement *after the verb.*

The three sentence elements—the subject, the verb, and the complement—form the basic center of the sentence. All other sentence elements expand or unite these elements in some way.

The combinations of verbs and complements produce different types of basic sentence patterns. The chart on the following page gives the most common patterns.

Sentence Patterns			Comments	Examples of Verbs
Subject	Verb	Complement		
The girls S	laughed. V_{int}	———	The verb expresses an action but does not take an object. The verb is called an *intransitive* verb.	*walk, talk, sleep, disappear, exist, run*
John S	kissed V_{tr}	Mary. O	A verb taking an object is called a *transitive verb*. *Mary* is the *object* of the verb. Note that *John* and *Mary* refer to different people. (If an action is involved, the object is the "receiver" of the action.)	*love, carry, kill, throw, discuss, eat, drink, take, bring, bake, cook, paint, write*
Mary S	is V_{link}	a girl. PN (predicate noun)	Verbs like *is* are *linking* verbs. The subject *Mary* is the same person as the predicate noun *girl*. The predicate noun is called a *subjective complement*; it is a word in the predicate that has the same reference as the subject.	*be (is, am, are, was, were), become, remain*
Mary S	seems V_{link}	happy. PA (predicate adjective)	Verbs like *seem* are *linking* verbs. The predicate adjective *happy* describes the subject *Mary*. The predicate adjective is also called a *subjective complement*. *Note*: Linking verbs are all intransitive but they must be followed by subjective complements.	*be, become, seem, remain, look, appear, taste, smell*

GRAMMAR REVIEW AND PRACTICE

EXERCISE 1

In the blank spaces, label the verbs and the complements.

Label the verbs:

		Label the complements:
V$_{int}$	*intransitive* verb—does not take an object	
V$_t$	*transitive* verb—takes an object O	*object* (different from the subject—often the "receiver" of an action)
V$_{link}$	*linking* verb—takes a predicate noun or a predicate adjective that refers back to the subject (subjective complement) PN PA	*predicate noun* (the same person or thing as the subject) *predicate adjective* (describes the subject)

Subject	Verb (V$_{intr}$, V$_{tr}$, V$_{link}$)		Complement (O, PN, PA)	
1. The mailman	delivered	(V$_{tr}$)	the letter.	(O)
2. The police	arrested	( )	the thief.	( )
3. Her daughter	is	( )	a nurse.	( )
4. The baby	cried.	( )	_____	
5. The woman	seems	( )	angry.	( )
6. Children	like	( )	candy.	( )
7. The milk	tastes	( )	sour.	( )
8. The artist	painted	( )	a picture.	( )
9. The mob	rioted.	( )	_____	
10. That woman	is	( )	an actress.	( )
11. The students	were	( )	tired.	( )

There are two small groups of verbs that take not one, but *two* complements.

1. The complements can be *indirect object* and *direct object*.

     John   gave   Mary   flowers.   (The two objects, *Mary* and *flowers*,
     S   V$_{tr}$ IO   DO   do not have the same reference.)

The indirect object here tells who received something (*Mary*).
The direct object (DO) tells what is received (*flowers*). It follows the
     indirect object.

UNDERSTANDING SENTENCES

Such complements can also be rephrased as: *John gave flowers to Mary.*

2. The complements can be *direct object* and *objective complement.*

The company	considers	that *man*	a *genius.*[1]	(The two objects,
S	V$_{tr}$	DO	OC	*man* and *genius*, have the same reference.)

The objective complement is usually a noun (*genius*), but sometimes it is an adjective: *I consider that man* **great.** It stands in the same relationship to the direct object as the subjective complement stands to the subject (*That man is a genius*).

EXERCISE 2

The following sentences contain two complements after each verb. In the blank spaces, label these complements:

IO   DO   (indirect object, direct object), after verbs like *give, write, lend, take, send, teach*

DO   OC   (direct object, objective complement), after verbs like *make, consider, elect, choose, select, appoint*

If you have an IO, restate the sentence using a *to* phrase.

1. The nurse brought   the patient (_IO_)   some medicine (_DO_).
   Also: The nurse brought some medicine to the patient.

2. The court appointed   her uncle (_DO_)   guardian (_OC_).

3. The foreman sent   his boss (_____)   a letter (_____).

4. We consider   that man (_____)   a liar (_____).

5. The bank lent   the man (_____)   some money (_____).

6. A substitute taught   the class (_____)   geography (_____).

7. The people elected   Lincoln (_____)   president (_____).

8. The author wrote   his publisher (_____)   a letter (_____).

---

[1] *As* often appears before an objective complement: *The court appointed her uncle* **as** *guardian.*

GRAMMAR REVIEW AND PRACTICE

9. The president appointed his brother (_____) chairman (_____).

10. The children made their teacher (_____) angry (_____).

EXERCISE 3

The basic sentence patterns that have already been given may be used in four types of sentences.

STATEMENTS: The Johnsons bought a new home.
QUESTIONS: Did the Johnsons buy a new home?
 When did the Johnsons buy a new home?
COMMANDS
(OR REQUESTS): Close the window.
EXCLAMATIONS: How quickly the police arrived. (*or* !)
 What a beautiful home you have. (*or* !)

Change the following statements into questions. Begin each question with the word to the left of the statement. Reverse the position of the subject and the first part of the verb (the auxiliary). For most verbs with no auxiliary, *do, does,* or *did* must be added to start the question.

1. (Does) His wife cleans the house every day.
   Does his wife clean the house every day?

2. (Why) We must leave soon.
   Why must we leave soon?

3. (Do) The children go to bed early.

4. (Are His students are taking a test today.

5. (Does) He takes his medicine at night.

6. (Has) The train has arrived late.

7. (Did) His wife washed the dishes.

8. (When) They are coming.

9. (Why) His friend stole the money.

UNDERSTANDING SENTENCES

10. (Where)   Their father went yesterday.
_____

11. (How)   The company will get the loan.
_____

12. (Why)   I should help you.
_____

EXERCISE 4

Change the following statements into exclamations. Start the exclamation with *how* or *what* plus the italicized words. Use normal subject–verb order after the exclamatory part of the sentence.

1. This dress is *expensive*.
   How expensive this dress is. (or !)
   (*How* is required if the exclamatory phrase ends with an *adjective* [*expensive*] or with an *adverb* [**How quickly** *she types.*])

2. This is *an expensive dress*.
   What an expensive dress this is. (or !)
   (*What* [a] is required if the exclamatory phrase ends with a *noun* [*dress*].)

3. The cost of living is *high* in this city.
_____

4. She's *a wonderful teacher*.
_____

5. Our teacher is *wonderful*.
_____

6. You look *handsome* today.
_____

7. We are having *good weather*.
_____

8. She sings *beautifully*.
_____

9. The orchestra is playing *beautiful music*.
_____

10. His memory is *bad*.
_____

11. He drives *carelessly*.
_____

12. He told us *an amusing story*.
_____

UNIT TWO
Parts of Speech

English words are classified grammatically according to the kind of use, or function, they have in a sentence. Each of the classifications by function is called a *part of speech*. Thus, for example, subjects, objects, and most complements are given the part-of-speech name *nouns*. Nouns, together with *verbs,* form the central core of the sentence. This core may be diagramed thus:

Sentence: **Unambitious students frequently take easy programs in college.**

(Part of Speech)	Noun	Verb	Noun
central core ⟶	**students**	**take**	**programs**
(function)	subject	(center of sentence)	object

The words in the central core may be modified (meaning *limited* or *described*) by other words. Those words modifying nouns are called *adjectives,* and those modifying verbs are called *adverbs*.

The modifying words may be diagramed as shown on the following page:

PARTS OF SPEECH

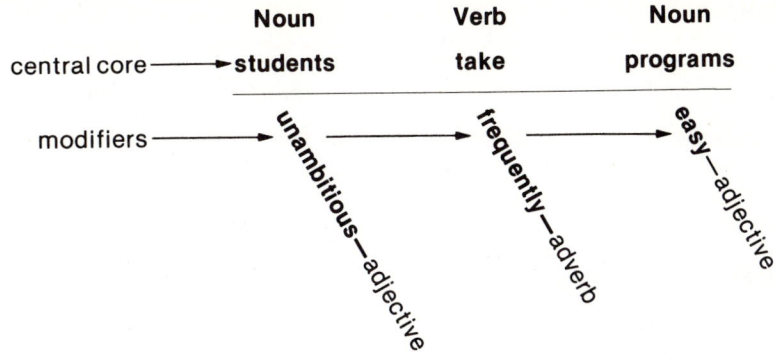

Other words in a sentence have a joining function. There are two parts of speech that have this function: the *conjunction* and the *preposition*.

1. A *conjunction* connects words or word groups that have the same function (coordinate conjunctions).[1]

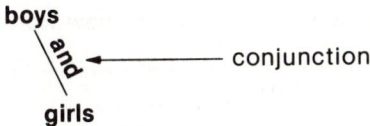

2. A *preposition* connects a noun to another word.

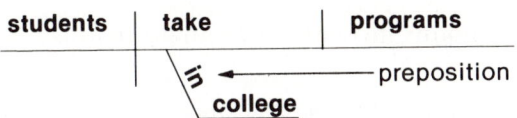

Here we see another important function of a noun: the word *college* is considered the object of the preposition *in*.

One other part of speech, the *pronoun,* often acts as a substitute for a noun. Thus, substituting pronouns for the nouns in the central core of the sentence we have been working with, we get:

they	take	them

One type of word that is traditionally also classified as a part of speech, although it has no real function in a sentence, is the *interjection*. The interjection is a word that expresses feeling of some kind such as surprise, disgust, pain—words like *oh, well, ouch*.

---

[1] The *coordinate* conjunction (*and, or, nor, but, so, for,* and *yet*) is only one type of conjunction. The other type, the *subordinate* conjunction, makes one group of words dependent on another. This type will be taken up in the chapter on complex structures, particularly in the discussion of adverbial clauses.

GRAMMAR REVIEW AND PRACTICE

EXERCISE 1

A. Diagram the following sentences for the core and their modifiers. Give the part of speech for each word in the diagram. (Omit *a, an, the,* and *their.*)

Example: A clever thief easily stole the famous painting from the museum.

	Noun	**Verb**	**Noun**
(central core)	thief	stole	painting
(modifiers)	clever—adjective	easily—adverb	famous—adjective

1. Their English teacher carefully wrote the new words on the blackboard.
2. The old man slowly lifted the heavy packages from the floor.
3. An unknown author unexpectedly wrote a successful novel about the war.
4. An angry reader wrote a long letter to the newspaper.

B. Underline the nouns in Exercise 1A that are functioning as objects of prepositions.

Example: A clever thief easily stole the famous painting from the <u>museum.</u>

    The parts of speech usually have definite positions in the sentence according to their functions. For example, a noun subject appears before its verb, and an adjective modifier appears before its noun. There are also certain types of words that signal the part of speech that will follow: for example, *the* is a "marker" that signals a following noun, *very* "marks" a following adjective or adverb.
    In addition, four parts of speech—nouns, adjectives, verbs, and adverbs—often have special forms that identify them as such. One type of ending, for instance, signals certain grammatical meanings: thus *-s* signifies "more than one" with a noun, *-ed* signifies past time with a verb. Another type of ending changes one part of speech into another: thus, *-ment* added to the verb *arrange* changes it to the noun *arrangement;* *-ous* added to the noun *fame* changes the word to the adjective *famous.*
    In the rest of this unit, nouns, adjectives, verbs, and adverbs will be identified according to their physical characteristics of function, position, form, and markers.

PARTS OF SPEECH

IDENTIFYING CHARACTERISTICS OF NOUNS

Function	Position	
subject	before the verb	**Children** *like animals.*
object of the verb	after the verb	Direct object: *Children like* **animals.**
		Indirect object: *He brought his* **children** *a dog.*
object of a preposition	after a preposition (words like *of, in, on, at, to, from, with*)	*Children are fond of* **animals.**
subjective complement	after a linking verb (especially *be*)	*The bear is an* **animal.**
objective complement	after a verb like *elect, choose, name, consider, make*	*We consider Mr. Smith a good* **candidate.**
appositive	after another noun (usually between commas)	*Dr. Jones, a famous* **surgeon,** *is retiring.*
Form		
inflectional (for grammar)	-*s*, regular plural	*girls*
	'*s*, possessive	*girl's, girls'*
derivational	special noun endings	-*ment, -tion, -(il)ity, -ence* or *-ance, -ness, -ist, -ism, -er,* or *-or, -hood, -ship, -ing, -th, -ure, -al,* etc.
Markers (modify the nouns)	1. *determiners* (introduce the phrase that ends with the noun. These represent a special class of adjectives.)	
	articles	*a, the*
	demonstratives	*this, that, these, those*
	possessives	*my, John's,* etc.
	definite numbers	*four, seventh,* etc.
	indefinite quantity	*many, some, several,* etc.
	2. *descriptive adjectives*	*beautiful, famous, useless,* etc.

GRAMMAR REVIEW AND PRACTICE

EXERCISE 2

Underline the *nouns* in the following sentences. Give the special characteristics that identify these nouns—function, position, form, markers.

    Example: The bookkeeper keeps careful records.

                    The <u>bookkeeper</u> keeps careful <u>records</u>.

	Bookkeeper	Records
Function	subject	object of the verb
Position	before the verb *keeps*	after the verb *keeps*
Form	*-er* noun ending	*-s* ending for the plural
Marker	the article *the*	descriptive adjective *careful*

1. Because of his illness, the professor announced his resignation.
2. Alice, the new typist, has great intelligence.
3. The university will mail the students their grades.
4. The chief requirement for this position is reliability.
5. The members elected Mary treasurer.

PARTS OF SPEECH

IDENTIFYING CHARACTERISTICS OF ADJECTIVES

Function	modify a noun or pronoun	
Position	before the noun	*a **pleasant** surprise*
	in the predicate (after a linking verb (*be, seem, appear, look*, etc.) as a subjective complement:	
	modifying a *noun* subject	*The day is very **pleasant**.*
	modifying a *pronoun* subject	*He is very **pleasant**.*
	in the predicate after a verb taking an objective complement (*keep, make, consider*)	*I consider him very **pleasant**.*
	after a special pronoun ending in *-thing, -one, -body*.	*He wants something **pleasant**.*
Form		
inflectional (for grammar)	*-er, -est* for comparison	*tal**ler**, tal**lest***
derivational	special adjective endings	*-ous, -ive, -ful, -less, -al, -ible* or *-able, -ent* or *-ant, -ing, -ed, -ic(al), -y, -some, -ish, -ile, -ly, -worthy*, etc.
Markers	adverbs of degree	*very, quite, extremely,* etc.
	adverbs for comparison (correspond to *-er, -est* inflectional endings)	*more, most* *less, least*

GRAMMAR REVIEW AND PRACTICE

EXERCISE 3

Underline the *adjectives* in the following sentences. Give the special characteristics that identify these adjectives—function, position, form, markers. (Omit the determiners, *the, their, his.*)

    Example: He looks very handsome in his uniform.

                         He looks very <u>handsome</u> in his uniform.

                  handsome: Function—modifies the pronoun subject *he* (as a subjective complement)
Position—in the predicate after the linking verb *looks*
Form—adjective ending *-some*
Marker—an adverb of degree, *very*

1. The friendly crowd cheered their political leaders.
2. His complete lack of respect for his hard-working parents was quite noticeable.
3. The nosy reporters made the famous actor very angry.
4. The president appears unhappy about the latest developments.
5. Everything enjoyable is either fattening or immoral.

IDENTIFYING CHARACTERISTICS OF VERBS

Function	center of sentence	
Position	usually:	
	after the subject	
	(except in questions)	*Children **like** toys.*
	before the complement	*She **is** a student.*
Form		
inflectional	-*s*, for third person singular	*he walk**s***
(for grammar)	-*ed* for: past tense	*he walk**ed***
	past participle	*he has walk**ed***
	-*ing* for: present participle	*he is walk**ing***
derivational	special verb endings	*-ize, -ify, -en, -ate*
	special verb prefixes	*en-, be-*
Markers	auxiliaries introduce the verb and are part of the verb	*be, have, will, shall, can, may, must,* etc.

EXERCISE 4

Underline the *verbs* in the following sentences. Include the auxiliaries. Give the form and markers that identify these verbs.[2]

Example: The arrangements for the dinner will be discussed tomorrow.
The arrangements for the dinner <u>will be discussed</u> tomorrow.
will be discussed: Form—*-ed* verb ending
Markers—the auxiliaries *will be*

1. His wife often talks too much.
2. They may reorganize the company.
3. The merchandise can be shipped immediately.
4. The strikers have been picketing for over a week.
5. Has the plane arrived yet?
6. The highway is being widened.

---

[2] For this exercise on verbs, it is not useful to include their function, since all verbs function as the center of the sentence, or the position, since verbs usually appear between the subject and the complement.

GRAMMAR REVIEW AND PRACTICE

IDENTIFYING CHARACTERISTICS OF ADVERBS

Function	modify a verb	walk **quickly**
	modify an adjective or another adverb (often as an adverb or degree)	a **very** quick walker walk **very** quickly
	modify the whole sentence	**Fortunately,** the plan worked.
	modify all parts of speech, as intensifiers	**Even** the children enjoyed the concert. (Even modifies the noun children.)
Position	initial	**Sometimes** she watches television.
	midposition (with the verb)	She **sometimes** watches television. She has **sometimes** watched television.
	final	She watches television **sometimes.**
Form	derivational	mostly -ly added to adjectives—indicates manner
		also: suffixes -ward (backward), -wise (otherwise), -where (somewhere)
		Some one- or two-syllable adverbs have the same form as adjectives: late, early, fast, slow, hard (meaning with great effort)
Markers (same as for adjectives)	adverbs of degree	very, quite, too, extremely, etc.
	adverbs for comparison	more, most; less, least

PARTS OF SPEECH

EXERCISE 5

Underline the *adverbs* in the following sentences. Give the special characteristics that identify the adverbs—function, position, form, markers. (For this exercise, consider adverbs of degree like *very, quite, extremely* only as markers of adjectives or other adverbs.)

 Example: She dances very gracefully.
 She dances very <u>gracefully</u>.
 gracefully: Function—modifies the verb *dances*
 Position—final position
 Form—ends in *-ly*
 Marker—*very*

1. They very frequently go to the movies on Friday night.
2. He was severely burned over half his body.
3. Recently she has been having trouble with her skin.
4. Obviously he was extremely uncomfortable.
5. Some students started school quite late, so they worked hard to catch up with the others.

UNIT THREE
Complex Structures

A sentence may be changed in such a way that it can be placed within another sentence. This changed sentence is a complex structure that can function as a *noun,* an *adjective,* or an *adverb* in the sentence where it is inserted.

If the complex structure keeps the full subject and predicate of the original sentence, the structure is called a *clause.* If the change involves a reduction from the full subject–predicate, the structure is called a *phrase.* Every complex structure is thus either a clause or a phrase.

The complex structures that will be given in this chapter cover most of the basic grammatical structures in the English language. They will be presented under the headings of *noun structures, adjective structures,* and *adverb structures.*

NOUN STRUCTURES (NOMINALS)

Like nouns, nominals serve as subjects, objects, complements, or appositives within a sentence.

Four types of noun structures are illustrated on the next page. The examples are all *subjects* in their sentences.

COMPLEX STRUCTURES

That she punished (or **should punish**) **the children so unfairly** *is inexcusable.*	**Noun Clause** contains a full subject and predicate
For her to punish the children so unfairly *is inexcusable.*	**Infinitive Phrase** the verb is in infinitive form (*to* plus the name of the verb) the original subject is often in a *for* phrase before the infinitive.
Her punishing the children so unfairly *is inexcusable.*	**Gerund Phrase** the verb is in *-ing* participial form the original subject is in possessive form
Her unfair punishment of the children *is inexcusable.*	**Abstract Noun Phrase** the original verb is in noun form the original subject is in possessive form the original object is in an *of* phrase

EXERCISE 1

Replace each sentence in parentheses with a noun structure that can serve as the subject of the rest of the sentence.

In some of the sentences, a less formal alternative for a nominal structure is an *it* construction which permits the nominal subject to be placed in the predicate.

    It is important *that they receive more money at once.* (noun clause)
    It is important *for them to receive more money at once.* (infinitive phrase)

Some alternative *it* constructions that sound natural are included in this exercise.

1. (He violated the law) was surprising.

    noun clause *That he violated the law was surprising.*

    or It *was surprising that he violated the law.*

    infinitive phrase *For him to violate the law was surprising.*

    gerund phrase *His violating the law was surprising.*

    abstract noun phrase *His violation of the law was surprising.*

GRAMMAR REVIEW AND PRACTICE

2. (They lost their only son) was a great tragedy.
   noun clause _____
   _____
   or It _____
   infinitive phrase _____
   or It _____
   gerund phrase _____
   abstract noun phrase _____

3. (They executed all the prisoners) came as a great shock to the world.
   noun clause _____
   _____
   or It _____
   infinitive phrase _____
   gerund phrase _____
   abstract noun phrase _____

4. (Her friend criticized his benefactors) surprised her.
   noun clause _____
   _____
   or It _____
   infinitive phrase _____
   gerund phrase _____
   abstract noun phrase _____

5. (The patient recovered so quickly from his illness) amazed his doctor.
   noun clause _____
   or It _____
   infinitive phrase _____
   gerund phrase _____
   abstract noun phrase _____

COMPLEX STRUCTURES

6. (The city dismissed all the striking firemen) seems unfair.
   noun clause _____

   _or_ It _____

   infinitive phrase _____

   _or_ It¹ _____

   gerund phrase _____

   abstract noun phrase _____

NOUN CLAUSES

The types of noun clauses are shown in the chart on the following page, along with the words that introduce these clauses.

---

[1] If the infinitive phrase subject comes in predicate position, there is sometimes a choice between *for* or *of* to introduce the phrase.

Noun Clause Derived From	Introductory Conjunction (subordinate)	Function of Clause	Examples
1. a statement *Coffee grows in Brazil.*	that	subject subject after *it* subjective complement object of verb appositive	***That coffee grows in Brazil** is well known to all.* *It is well known **that coffee grows in Brazil.** (less formal)* *My understanding is **that coffee grows in Brazil.*** *I know **(that) coffee grows in Brazil.*** *His belief **that coffee grows in Brazil** is correct.*
2. a question a. expecting yes or no answer *Will he get the money?*	whether (or not) also if	subject subjective complement object of verb object of preposition	***Whether (or not) he gets the money** doesn't concern me.* *The question is **whether he will get the money.*** *Do you know **whether (or if) he will get the money?*** *We were concerned about **whether he would get the money.***
b. interrogative word question *How will he get the money?*	who what which when where why how	subject subjective complement object of verb object of preposition	***How he gets the money** is his own affair.* *The question is **how he will get the money.*** *I don't know **how he will get the money.*** *We were concerned about **how he would get the money.***
3. a request *Write the letter soon.*	that	object of verb	*He suggested **that I write the letter soon.***
4. an exclamation *What a pretty girl she is!*	what how	object of verb object of preposition	*I hadn't realized **what a pretty girl she was.*** *We talked about **what a pretty girl she was.***

From Marcella Frank, *Modern English: Exercises for Non-native Speakers, Part Two: Sentences and Complex Structures* (Englewood Cliffs, N.J.: Prentice-Hall, 1972), p. 61. Reprinted by permission.

COMPLEX STRUCTURES

Punctuation of noun clauses

Commas are not used with noun clause subjects or objects.

NOUN CLAUSE
SUBJECT: *That he was proud of his talented wife* was quite evident.

NOUN CLAUSE
OBJECT: All his friends knew *that he was proud of his talented wife.*

The question mark is not retained in noun clauses made from questions (indirect questions).

QUESTION: Where do you live?
NOUN CLAUSE: He asked me *where I lived.*

Word order in noun clauses

In noun clauses from questions, normal subject–predicate order is used.

QUESTION: How *did the thieves enter?*
NOUN CLAUSE: The police are puzzled about how *the thieves entered.*

If a question beginning with *who* or *what* contains a form of the independent verb *be* plus a noun or a pronoun, this verb is placed at the *end* of the noun clause.

QUESTION: What *is* the address of the publisher?
NOUN CLAUSE: He asked me what the address of the publisher *was.*

Verb forms in noun clauses

If the verb in the main part of the sentence is in the past tense, the verb in the noun clause is usually past also (sequence of tenses), especially in formal English.

PRESENT
MAIN VERB: The interviewer *says* that he *will see* the applicant soon.

PAST
MAIN VERB: The interviewer *said* that he *would see* the applicant soon.

After verbs like *suggest, recommend, advise,* and *command,* the verb is in the *to*-less infinitive form, which may be preceded by the auxiliary *should.*

The doctor recommended that he (*should*) *take* a long rest.

GRAMMAR REVIEW AND PRACTICE

EXERCISE 2

Combine the following sets of sentences so that the word *this* in one sentence is replaced by a *noun clause* made from the other sentence. Note where it is also possible to use *it* constructions with noun clause subjects.

1. They are disobeying the law.
   This is quite evident.

   That they are disobeying the law is quite evident.

   or *It is quite evident that they are disobeying the law.*

2. His wife asked him *this*.
   "Why did you lie to me?"

   His wife asked him why he had lied (informal— *lied*) *to her.*

3. He asked me *this*.
   "Can anyone enter the contest?"

   He asked me whether (or *if*) *anyone could enter the contest.*

4. *This* is very encouraging.
   The child's fever has gone down.

5. Will he come or not?
   This was still uncertain.

6. He said *this*.
   "I don't understand your question."

7. We don't know *this*.
   Whom will the agency send us?

8. I can't decide *this*.
   Should I go or not?[2]

9. He asked me *this*.
   Where is the post office?

10. I inquired about *this*.
    When does the plane for Los Angeles leave?

11. Her parents asked her *this*.
    "What is the name of your teacher?"

---

[2] This noun clause can also have an infinitive structure: *I can't decide whether **to go** or not.*

COMPLEX STRUCTURES

ADJECTIVE STRUCTURES (ADJECTIVALS)

Like adjectives, adjectivals modify nouns. However, unlike simple adjectives, which come before a noun, adjectivals usually appear *after* a noun.

The types of adjective structures are given below.

Noun	Adjective Structure	Type of Structure
students	who are anxious to enter the university	**Adjective Clause** has a full subject and predicate introduced by *who* (for a person), *which* (for a thing), or *that* (for either a person or a thing)
homes	which are large enough for big families	
students	anxious to enter the university	**Adjective Phrase** begins with a descriptive adjective like *anxious* or *large*
houses	large enough for big families	
students	sitting in the front row	**Participial Phrase** begins with the *-ing* participle or the *-ed* participle)[3]
houses	located near the park	
students	in the front row	**Prepositional Phrase** begins with a preposition like *in, on, at, with, near, from, of, to* and ends with a noun or a pronoun
houses	near the park	

EXERCISE 3

Change the *second* sentence to the required adjective structure and place the structure after the noun it belongs to.

1. The money _____ was given to the poor.
   It was collected from the club members.

   adjective clause: The money *which (or that) was collected from the club members* was given to the poor.

   participial phrase: The money *collected from the club members* was given to the poor.

---

[3] In this book, the term *-ed* participle is used to include all irregular participles (tear, tore, **torn**).

GRAMMAR REVIEW AND PRACTICE

2. The person _____ will be punished.
   The person is responsible for the damage.
   adjective clause: The person *who is responsible for the damage* will be punished.
   adjective phrase: The person *responsible for the damage* will be punished.

3. A volcano _____ may erupt again.
   The volcano has been dormant for many years.
   adjective clause: A volcano _____ may erupt again.
   adjective phrase: A volcano _____ may erupt again.

4. The students _____ could not hear the professor.
   They were sitting in the rear of the lecture hall.
   adjective clause: The students _____ could not hear the professor.
   participial phrase: The students _____ could not hear the professor.
   prepositional phrase: The students _____ could not hear the professor.

5. A boy _____ may never become a mature, responsible adult.
   The boy is spoiled by his parents.
   adjective clause: A boy _____ may never become a mature, responsible adult.
   participial phrase: A boy _____ may never become a mature, responsible adult.

6. The jewelry _____ was found by the police.
   The jewelry had been stolen from their neighbor's house.
   adjective clause: The jewelry _____ was found by the police.
   participial phrase: The jewelry _____ was found by the police.

7. That gentleman _____ is an old friend of my father's.
   He is standing near the window.
   adjective clause: That gentleman _____ is an old friend of my father's.
   participial phrase: That gentleman _____ is an old friend of my father's.
   prepositional phrase: That gentleman _____ is an old friend of my father's.

COMPLEX STRUCTURES

Adjective clauses

An adjective clause[4] contains a full subject and predicate which modifies a noun or a pronoun. The introductory word in the clause (called a *relative pronoun*) may be the subject or the object in the clause. *Who* is used for a person, *which* for a thing, and *that* for either a person or a thing.

Function of Relative Pronoun	Relative Pronoun	Examples
Subject	who (or that)	The student **who** (or **that**) **is making all that noise** is a troublemaker.
	which (or that)	The chair **which** (or **that**) **needs to be repaired** is over there.
Object of Verb	whom (or that)	The student **whom** (or **that**) **our teacher is scolding** is a troublemaker.
	which (or that)	The chair **which** (or **that**) **we ordered last week** hasn't arrived yet.
Object of Preposition	whom	The student **to whom our teacher is talking** is a troublemaker.
	which	The chair **on which I'm sitting** is very comfortable.

As in questions, informal usage permits:

1. The object *whom* to be reduced to *who:*

    The student *who* our teacher is scolding is a troublemaker.

2. The preposition to come at the end of the construction:

    the student whom our teacher is talking *to;* the chair which I'm sitting *on*

In such cases too, *who* may replace *whom* informally.

Informal usage also permits the omission of relative pronouns used as objects of verbs, or as objects separated from their prepositions.

The student our teacher is scolding is a troublemaker.
The chair I'm sitting on is very comfortable.

Parenthetic phrases like *I know, we assume, it is believed* do not affect the form of the relative pronoun.

A man *who* the police believe stole the money has already been arrested. (*Who* is the subject of *stole* in the adjective clause. *The police believe* is regarded as a parenthetic element in the clause.)

[4] Adjective clauses are also called *relative clauses.*

GRAMMAR REVIEW AND PRACTICE

Whose is a possessive adjective referring to either a person or a thing in an adjective clause.

The student *whose* books were stolen is quite upset.

A building *whose* foundation is not strong may not be able to withstand a hurricane.

Adjective clauses may also be introduced by *when* or *where*.

June is the month *when* many couples get married. (A time word precedes *when*; *in which* may also be used here.)

The house *where* he was born has been torn down. (A place word precedes *where*; *in which* may also be used here.)

EXERCISE 4

Use *who, whom, which,* or *whose*. Observe formal usage. Note where the relative pronoun may be omitted in the adjective clauses.

1. I need to find a book _____ gives the basic principles of biology.
2. The man _____ car was stolen reported the theft to the police.
3. The chair on _____ the cat is sleeping is the best one in the house.
4. The actress _____ plays the leading role suddenly became sick.
5. The exact day on _____ the murder was committed is not known.
6. The building in _____ they live is going to be sold.
7. The child _____ the teacher was praising hung his head in embarrassment.
8. The lawyer is asking that all the demonstrators _____ were arrested yesterday be released.
9. There's no woman in the world _____ he really thinks is good enough for him.
10. The police came to see the people _____ house had been broken into.

EXERCISE 5

Change the sentence within parentheses into an adjective clause and place the clause after the noun it belongs to. Note the choices that are possible for the introductory word in the clause.

1. The music (the orchestra is rehearsing it now) is by Beethoven.
   The music (which, that, or nothing) the orchestra is rehearsing now is by Beethoven.

COMPLEX STRUCTURES

2. The jewelry disappeared from the drawer (she always keeps it in this drawer).
   The jewelry disappeared from the drawer (where or *in which) she always keeps it.*
   or *The jewelry disappeared from the drawer (which, that,* or nothing) *she always keeps it in.*

3. The children's parents are unable to raise the money (the kidnapper is demanding the money).

4. The costumes (they were needed for the play) got lost.

5. The man (his money had been stolen) did not report the theft to the police.

6. The day (they were to leave on this day) finally arrived.

7. She paid her uncle the money (she had borrowed it from him).

8. The museum (the famous *Mona Lisa* is located in this museum) is the Louvre.

9. I have two important phone calls (I must make them).[5]

Punctuation of adjective structures

If the adjective structure identifies or narrows down the noun it modifies, the structure is not set off by commas.

> A state *(which is) located in the South* produces peanuts.
> (*State* is a general class word which is narrowed down by the adjective structure.)

If the noun is already identified, especially if the noun is a proper noun (a name), the adjective structure is set off by commas.

> Georgia, *(which is) located in the South,* produces peanuts.

Commas are also required with the adjective structure if the noun represents only one member of a class.

---

[5] In this sentence, an alternative form for the adjective clause is the infinitive: *I have two important calls* **to make.**

GRAMMAR REVIEW AND PRACTICE

Their mother, who loves them dearly, is trying not to spoil them. (They have only one mother.)

but: A mother who loves her children will try not to spoil them. (*Mother* here represents an entire class which is narrowed down by the adjective structure.)

EXERCISE 6

Change the words in parentheses into adjective structures and rewrite the sentence. Use commas around these structures if they do not further identify the noun, especially if the noun is a proper noun.

1. Hong Kong (it, know, Jewel of the Pacific) is a British Crown Colony.
   Hong Kong, (which is) known as the Jewel of the Pacific, is a British Crown Colony.

2. Children (they, play, ball, in the street) must watch out for cars.

3. Their eldest child (he, play, ball, in the street) got hit by a car.

4. A country (it, know, fine coffee production) is trying to diversify its industries.

5. Colombia (it, know, fine coffee production) is trying to diversify its industries.

6. Hawaii (it, locate, middle, Pacific) is a meeting place of East and West.

7. An island (it, locate, middle, Pacific) is a meeting place of East and West.

8. A compound (it, consist, oxygen and hydrogen) is water.

9. Water (it, consist, oxygen and hydrogen) is a compound.

COMPLEX STRUCTURES

ADVERB STRUCTURES (ADVERBIALS)

Like adverbs, most adverbials modify verbs or the whole sentence. Unlike noun and adjective structures, which have fixed positions in a sentence, adverb structures are often more loosely attached to a sentence.

Two common types of adverb structures are given below.

Because he is selfish, the young man has very few friends.	Adverbial Clause has a full subject and predicate begins with a conjunction such as *because, although, while, if*
Because of his selfishness, the young man has very few friends.	Prepositional Phrase begins with a preposition such as *because of, in spite of, during, in case of* ends with a noun or pronoun

Position of adverb structures

Many adverb structures, like adverbs, have three possible positions.

> INITIAL POSITION: *Because he is selfish,* the young man has very few friends.
>
> MIDPOSITION: The young man, *because he is selfish,* has very few friends. (This position is less common.)
>
> FINAL POSITION: The young man has very few friends *because he is selfish.*

Punctuation of adverb structures

The punctuation of adverb structures is somewhat flexible. Commas are more likely to be used with initial adverb structures than with final ones, especially if the initial structure is long. (See **Punctuation** in the Index of Usage and Rhetoric for further information about punctuating adverb structures.)

EXERCISE 7

Combine the sets of sentences so that the *first sentence* becomes (1) an adverbial clause, and (2) a prepositional phrase.

1. He was very careless.
   He made some bad mistakes.
     adverbial clause *Because he was very careless, he made some bad mistakes.*
     prepositional phrase *Because of his great carelessness, he made some bad mistakes.*

GRAMMAR REVIEW AND PRACTICE

2. He is very young.
   But the boy is already a talented musician.
   adverbial clause *Although he is very young,* [6] *the boy is already a talented musician.*
   prepositional phrase *In spite of his great youth, the boy is already a talented musician.*

3. The defendant refused to answer the questions.
   The judge sentenced him to a jail term.
   adverbial clause _____
   _____
   prepositional phrase _____
   _____

4. They were very poor.
   But they managed to save some money.
   adverbial clause _____
   _____
   prepositional phrase _____
   _____

5. She was irritated by her friend's remarks.
   However, she said nothing in reply.
   adverbial clause _____
   _____
   prepositional phrase[7] _____
   _____

6. She was generous with her friends.
   However, she did not spend money foolishly.
   adverbial clause _____
   _____
   prepositional phrase _____
   _____

7. The bridge was destroyed.
   The enemy couldn't advance any further.
   adverbial clause _____
   _____
   prepositional phrase _____
   _____

[6] This clause with *although* may also be reduced to *although very young*.
[7] In this sentence, *by* is replaced by *at*.

COMPLEX STRUCTURES

Adverbial clauses[8]

An adverbial clause contains a subject and a predicate introduced by a special word having a meaning such as cause, time, or condition. This introductory word is called a *subordinate conjunction* because the adverbial clause it introduces is considered as only a part of a sentence and must be attached to a main clause. The types of adverbial clauses are given below, along with the subordinate conjunctions that begin each kind of clause.

Type of Clause	Subordinate Conjunction Beginning the Clause		Examples
Time	when while since before after until as	as soon as as long as by the time (that) now that once	I can see you **when I finish my work.** She was reading a book **while the dinner was cooking.** I have not seen him **since he returned to the country.** They will leave **before you get here.** Abridgments of time clauses: **When** (or **While**) **young,** I looked at things differently. **When a boy,** I looked at things differently. She always sings **when doing her work.** Experience, **when dearly bought,** is seldom thrown away.
Place	where wherever		We live **where the road crosses the river.** Abridgments of place clauses: **Wherever possible,** the illustrations are taken from literature.
Cause	because since as now that whereas (legal)		He could not come **because** (or **since, as**) **he was ill.** **Now that he has passed the examination,** he can get his degree. *(continued)*

---

[8] From Marcella Frank, *Modern English: Exercises for Non-native Speakers, Part Two: Sentences and Complex Structures* (Englewood Cliffs, N.J.: Prentice-Hall, 1972), pp. 21-22. Reprinted by permission.

GRAMMAR REVIEW AND PRACTICE

Type of Clause	Subordinate Conjunction Beginning the Clause	Examples
Cause (cont.)	*inasmuch as* (formal) *as long as* *on account of the fact that* *owing to the fact that* *in view of the fact that* *because of the fact that* *due to the fact that* (informal)	**Whereas they have disobeyed the law,** they will be punished. **Inasmuch as no one was hurt because of his negligence,** the judge gave him a light sentence. **On account of** (or **owing to**) **the fact that the country was at war,** all the young men were drafted. Abridgments of cause clauses: It is an unpardonable insult, **since intentional.**
Condition	*if* *unless* *on condition that* *provided* } *providing* } *that* *in the event that* *in case that* *whether . . . or not*	**If it rains,** we won't have the picnic. We won't have the picnic **unless the weather is good.** We'll have the picnic **providing that it doesn't rain.** **In the event** (or **in case**) **(that) it rains,** the picnic will be postponed. Abridgments of conditional clauses: In contrary-to-fact conditions: Present—**Were I in your position,** I would take advantage of that offer. Past—**Had I known you were coming,** I would have met you at the station. Please come early **if possible.** This appliance will not work **unless properly attached.**
Contrast: concessive	*although* *though* *even though* *even if* *in spite of* } *despite* } *the fact that*	**Although** (or **Though**) **I felt very tired,** I tried to finish the work. **In spite of the fact that prices went down recently,** the company made a huge profit.

(*continued*)

126

COMPLEX STRUCTURES

Type of Clause	Subordinate Conjunctions Beginning the Clause	Examples
concessive (cont.)	notwithstanding (the fact) that (formal)	**Notwithstanding the fact that the government was weak at that time,** law and order were maintained.
		Abridgments of concession clauses:
		Although in a hurry, he stopped to help the boy.
		Although only a boy, he does a man's work.
		Although fond of his work, he wants to find a job that will be more challenging.
adversative	while where whereas	Some people spend their spare time reading, **while others watch television.**
Purpose	that in order that so (informal) so that for the purpose that	They climbed higher **that** (or **so that, in order that**) **they might get a better view.** He is saving his money **so that he can go to college.**
Result	so + adj. or adv. + that such (a) + noun + that so that	She is **so** pretty (adj.) **that she attracts a lot of attention.** She sang **so** beautifully (adv.) **that everyone applauded her performance.** She has **such** pretty hair (noun) **that we all enjoy looking at it.** It's **such a** hot day (sing. count. noun) **that I must go to the beach.** They climbed higher, **so that they got a better view.**
Comparison	as (not) so } + adj. or adv. + as -er more } + adj. or adv. + than	She works just **as** hard **as her sister works.** She doesn't work **so** (or **as**) hard **as her sister works.** She works harder **than her sister works.** Abridgments of comparison clauses (very common): She works **just as hard as her sister** (does). *(continued)*

127

GRAMMAR REVIEW AND PRACTICE

Type of Clause	Subordinate Conjunctions Beginning the Clause	Examples
Comparison (*cont.*)		She works harder **than her sister (does).**
Manner	as if as though (especially after *look, seem, act*)	He looks **as if he needs** (or **needed**) **more sleep.** He hasn't behaved **as a gentleman should behave.** Abridgment of manner clauses: He hasn't behaved **as a gentleman should.** He left the room **as though angry.** The clouds disappeared **as if by magic.** He raised his hand **as if to command silence.**

EXERCISE 8

Combine the sentences by replacing the italicized expressions in the second sentence with a subordinate conjunction at the beginning of the first sentence. More than one position is possible for the adverbial clauses.

A. *Adverbial clauses of time*—subordinate conjunctions *when, while, since, until, before, after* (Do *not* use a comma before the time clause in final position)

1. He was playing tennis.
 During this time he suffered a heart attack.
 <u>While he was playing tennis, he suffered a heart attack.</u> [9]
 or: <u>He suffered a heart attack while he was playing tennis.</u>

2. They made very careful preparations.
 Then they did the experiment.

3. His teacher encouraged him.
 Already he has been doing better work in class.

4. Gold was discovered in California in 1848.
 Up to this time the state had relatively few inhabitants.

---

[9] It is also possible to say *while playing tennis*. (Such a reduction of the clause can also occur after *before, after, since, when.*)

COMPLEX STRUCTURES

B. *Adverbial clauses of concession*—subordinate conjunctions *although, even though, though*

5. She dislikes housework.
   But she's trying her best to be a good cook.
   ___

6. He talks about his grandiose schemes.
   Yet he never seems to accomplish any of them.
   ___

7. He's studying much harder now.
   However, his grades in school are still poor.
   ___

C. *Adverbial clauses of cause*—subordinate conjunctions *because, since, as*

8. We have very little money now.
   So we have to do without the little luxuries we used to have.
   ___

9. There was a severe drought this year.
   Therefore, the crops have been very poor.
   ___

10. He has refused to accept any additional responsibilities on his job.
    For this reason, he will never be promoted.
    ___

D. *Adverbial clauses of condition*—subordinate conjunctions *if, unless, in case* (These conditional clauses require some changes in the verb forms of the first sentences.)

11. My wife may call the office.
    In this case, tell her I'll be back in an hour.
    ___

12. We must get new tires for the car.
    Otherwise, we may have an accident on the road.
    ___

13. Stop driving so fast.
    Or you'll get a ticket.
    ___

E. *Adversative adverbial clauses*—subordinate conjunctions *while, whereas*

14. Some people require very little sleep.
    But others need to have at least eight hours' sleep.
    ___

GRAMMAR REVIEW AND PRACTICE

15. The pace of life in the city is very fast.
    In the country, *on the other hand,* people move at a more leisurely pace.
    _____

16. The former mayor made very few public appearances.
    The present mayor, *however,* is often seen at parades, meetings, and other public functions.
    _____

Answers to Grammar Exercises

UNIT ONE—Understanding Sentences

Exercise 1   2. V_{tr} O   3. V_{link} PN   4. V_{int} ---   5. V_{link} PA   6. V_{tr} O   7. V_{link} PA   8. V_{tr} O   9. V_{int} ---   10. V_{link} PN   11. V_{link} PA

Exercise 2   3. IO DO   *Also:* The foreman sent a letter to his boss.   4. DO OC   5. IO DO   *Also:* The bank lent some money to the man.   6. IO DO   *Also:* A substitute taught geography to the class.   7. DO OC   8. IO DO   *Also:* The author wrote a letter to his publisher.   9. DO OC   10. DO OC

Exercise 3   3. Do the children go to bed early?   4. Are his students taking a test today?   5. Does he take his medicine at night?   6. Has the train arrived late?   7. Did his wife wash the dishes?   8. When are they coming?   9. Why did his friend steal the money?   10. Where did their father go yesterday?   11. How will the company get the loan?   12. Why should I help you?

Exercise 4   3. How high the cost of living is in this city.   4. What a wonderful teacher she is.   5. How wonderful our teacher is.   6. How handsome you look today.   7. What good weather we are having.   8. How beautifully she sings.   9. What beautiful music the orchestra is playing.   10. How bad his memory is.   11. How carelessly he drives.   12. What an amusing story he told us. (Also, an exclamation mark may be used at the end of each of these sentences.)

UNIT TWO—Parts of Speech

Exercise 1A

1.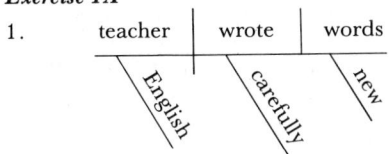

ANSWERS TO GRAMMAR EXERCISES

2.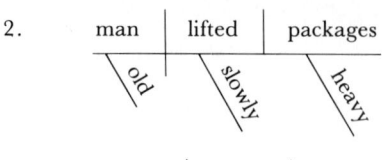

3.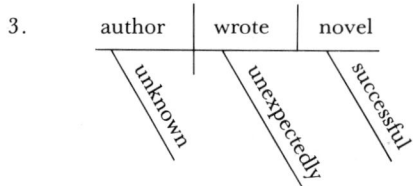

4. reader | wrote | letter
   (angry) (long)

Exercise 1B   1. *blackboard*   2. *floor*   3. *war*   4. *newspaper*

Exercise 2

1.	*illness*	*professor*	*resignation*
Function	object of preposition *because*	subject	object of the verb
Position	after the preposition	before the verb *announced*	after the verb *announced*
Form	*-ness* ending	*-or* ending	*-ation* ending
Marker	the determiner *his*	the article *the*	the determiner *his*
2.	*Alice*	*typist*	*intelligence*
Function	subject	appositive	object of the verb
Position	before the verb *has*	after another noun	after the verb *has*
Form	—	*-ist* ending	*-ence* ending
Marker	—	the article *the*, the adjective *new*	the adjective *great*
3.	*university*	*students*	*grades*
Function	subject	indirect object	direct object
Position	before the verb *will mail*	after the verb *will mail*	after the verb *will mail*
Form	*-ity* ending	*-s* ending (for plural)	*-s* ending (for plural)
Marker	the article *the*	the article *the*	the determiner *their*
4.	*requirement*	*position*	*reliability*
Function	subject	object of the preposition	predicate noun (subjective complement)
Position	before the verb *is*	after the preposition *for*	after the linking verb *is*
Form	*-ment* ending	*-tion* ending	*-ility* ending
Marker	the article *the*, descriptive adjective *chief*	*this*	—

ANSWERS TO GRAMMAR EXERCISES

5.	*members*	*Mary*	*treasurer*
Function	subject	direct object	objective complement
Position	before the verb *elected*	after the verb *elected*	after the verb *elected*
Form	-*s* ending (for plural)	—	-*er* ending
Marker	the article *the*	—	—

Exercise 3

1.	*friendly*	*political*	
Function	modifies the noun *crowd*	modifies the noun *leaders*	
Position	before the noun	before the noun	
Form	-*ly* ending	-*ical* ending	
Marker	—	—	
2.	*complete*	*hard-working*	*noticeable*
Function	modifies the noun *lack*	modifies the noun *parents*	predicate adjective (subjective complement) modifies *lack of respect*
Position	before the noun	before the noun	after the linking verb *was*
Form	—	-*ing* ending	-*able* ending
Marker	—	—	quite
3.	*nosy*	*famous*	*angry*
Function	modifies the noun *reporters*	modifies the noun *actor*	objective complement
Position	before the noun	before the noun	after the verb *made*
Form	-*y* ending	-*ous* ending	-*y* ending
Marker	—	—	very
4.	*unhappy*	*latest*	
Function	predicate adjective (subjective complement) modifies *president*	modifies the noun *developments*	
Position	after the linking verb *appears*	before the noun	
Form	—	-*est* ending	
Marker	—	—	
5.	*enjoyable*	*fattening*	*immoral*
Function	modifies the pronoun *everything*	predicate adjective (subjective complement)	predicate adjective (subjective complement)
Position	after the pronoun	after the linking verb *is*	after the linking verb *is*
Form	-*able* ending	-*ing* ending	—
Marker	—	—	—

Exercise 4

1.	*talks*
Form	-*s* ending
Marker	—
2.	*may reorganize*
Form	-*ize* ending
Marker	*may* auxiliary

ANSWERS TO GRAMMAR EXERCISES

3.   *can be shipped*
Form   *-ed* ending
Marker   auxiliaries *can be*

4.   *have been picketing*
Form   *-ing* ending
Marker   auxiliaries *have been*

5.   *has arrived*
Form   *-ed* ending
Marker   auxiliary *has*

6.   *is being widened*
Form   *-en, -ed* endings
Marker   auxiliaries *is being*

Exercise 5

1.   *frequently*
Function   modifies the verb *go*
Position   midposition, with the verb
Form   *-ly* ending
Marker   *-very*

2.   *severely*
Function   modifies the verb *was burned*
Position   midposition, with the verb
Form   *-ly* ending
Marker   —

3.   *Recently*
Function   modifies the whole sentence
Position   initial position
Form   *-ly* ending
Marker   —

4.   *Obviously*
Function   modifies the whole sentence
Position   initial position
Form   *-ly* ending
Marker   —

5.   *late*   *hard*
Function   modifies the verb *started*   modifies the verb *worked*
Position   final position   final position
Form   —   —
Marker   *quite*   —

UNIT THREE—Complex Structures

Exercise 1

2. *noun clause*—that they lost their only son; *infinitive phrase*—for them to lose their only son; *gerund phrase*—their losing their only son; *abstract noun phrase*—the loss of their only son.

3. *noun clause*—that they executed all the prisoners; *infinitive phrase*—for them to execute all

ANSWERS TO GRAMMAR EXERCISES

the prisoners; *gerund phrase*—their executing all the prisoners; *abstract noun phrase*—their execution of all the prisoners.

4. *noun clause*—that her friend criticized his benefactors; *infinitive phrase*—for her friend to criticize his benefactors; *gerund phrase*—her friend's criticizing his benefactors; *abstract noun phrase*—her friend's criticism of his benefactors.

5. *noun clause*—that the patient recovered so quickly from his illness; *infinitive phrase*—for the patient to recover so quickly from his illness; *gerund phrase*—the patient's recovering so quickly from his illness; *abstract noun phrase*—the patient's quick recovery from his illness.

6. *Noun clause*—that the city dismissed all the striking firemen; *infinitive phrase*—for the city to dismiss all the striking firemen seems unfair, It seems unfair for (*or* of) the city to dismiss all the striking firemen; *gerund phrase*—the city's dismissing all the striking firemen; *abstract noun phrase*—the city's dismissal of all the striking firemen.

Exercise 2

4. That the child's fever has gone down is very encouraging, *or* It is very encouraging that the child's fever has gone down.

5. Whether he would come or not was still uncertain, *or* It was still uncertain whether he would come or not.

6. He said that he didn't understand my question.

7. We don't know whom the agency will send us.

8. I can't decide whether I should go or not, *or* I can't decide whether to go or not.

9. He asked me where the post office was.

10. I inquired about when the plane for Los Angeles left.

11. Her parents asked her what the name of her teacher was.

Exercise 3

3. *adjective clause*—which has been dormant for many years; *adjective phrase*—dormant for many years.

4. *adjective clause*—who (*or* that) were sitting in the rear of the lecture hall; *participial phrase*—sitting in the rear of the lecture hall; *prepositional phrase*—in the rear of the lecture hall.

5. *adjective clause*—who (*or* that) is spoiled by his parents; *participial phrase*—spoiled by his parents.

6. *adjective clause*—which (*or* that) had been stolen from their neighbor's house; *participial phrase*—stolen from their neighbor's house.

7. *adjective clause*—who (*or* that) is standing near the window; *participial phrase*—standing near the window; *prepositional phrase*—near the window.

Exercise 4

1. which 2. whose 3. which 4. who 5. which 6. which 7. whom (may be omitted) 8. who 9. who 10. whose

Exercise 5

3. which, that, *or nothing* 4. which, that 6. when, on which 5. whose money 7. which, that, *or nothing* 8. where, in which 9. which, to make

Exercise 6

2. Children who (*or* that) play ball in the street . . . . ; Children playing ball in the street . . . .

ANSWERS TO GRAMMAR EXERCISES

3. Their eldest child, who was playing ball in the street, ... ; Their eldest child, playing ball in the street, ...

4. A country which (*or* that) is known for its fine coffee production . . . . ; A country known for its fine coffee production . . . .

5. Colombia, which is known for its fine coffee production, ... ; Colombia, known for its fine coffee production, ...

6. Hawaii, which is located in the middle of the Pacific, ... ; Hawaii, located in the middle of the Pacific, ...

7. An island which (*or* that) is located in the middle of the Pacific . . . . ; An island located in the middle of the Pacific . . . .

8. A compound which (*or* that) consists of oxygen and hydrogen . . . . ; A compound consisting of oxygen and hydrogen . . . .

9. Water, which consists of oxygen and hydrogen, ... ; Water, consisting of oxygen and hydrogen, ...

Exercise 7

3. *adverbial clause*—Because (*or* since, as) the defendant refused to answer the questions; *prepositional phrase*—Because of the defendant's refusal to answer the questions.

4. *adverbial clause*—Although (*or* even though, though) they were very poor; *prepositional phrase*—In spite of their great poverty.

5. *adverbial clause*—Although she was irritated by her friend's remarks; *prepositional phrase*—In spite of her irritation at her friend's remarks.

6. *adverbial clause*—Although she was generous with her friends; *prepositional phrase*—In spite of her generosity with her friends.

7. *adverbial clause*—Because the bridge was destroyed; *prepositional phrase*—Because of the destruction of the bridge.

Exercise 8

2. After they made or had made (*or* After making, having made) very careful preparations, ...

3. Since his teacher encouraged him, ...

4. Until (*or* Before) gold was discovered in California in 1848, ...

5. Although (even though, *or* though) she dislikes housework, ...

6. Although (even though, *or* though) he talks about his grandiose schemes, ...

7. Although (even though, *or* though) he's studying much harder now, ...

8. Because (since *or* as) we have very little money now, ...

9. Because (since *or* as) there was a severe drought this year, ...

10. Because (since *or* as) he has refused to accept any additional responsibilities on his job, ...

11. If (*or* in case) my wife calls the office, ...

12. If we don't get (*or* unless we get) new tires for the car, ...

13. If you don't stop (*or* unless you stop) driving so fast, ...

14. While (*or* whereas) some people require very little sleep, ...

15. While (*or* whereas) the pace of life in the city is very fast, ...

16. While (*or* whereas) the former mayor made very few public appearances, ...

Symbol Chart for Correction of Compositions

Note: starred symbols indicate more elementary types of faults.

* agree   *agreement.*   Make the verb singular or plural according to the main word in the subject.
   The architecture of these buildings *is* very interesting.
   If *each* or *every* is part of the subject, the verb must be singular.
   ***Everybody is coming* to the party.**

* ap   *apostrophe.*   An apostrophe has been incorrectly added or omitted. Apostrophes are used for contractions with auxiliaries (*who's = who is*) or for possessives of nouns (*the girl's hat*) but not for the possessive of pronouns (*its function, whose book*).

* art   *article.*   The article (*a, an, the*) is incorrect or omitted. Use an article with a singular countable noun. Do not use an article with a noncountable noun that stands alone (*I am studying history*). Use *the* if the noncountable noun is followed by a modifier (*the* history *of the United States*).

* C   *capital letter.*   Correct for capitalization. Use an initial capital letter for a word referring to nationality or religion (*an Italian custom; the Catholic religion*), a day of the week, a month, a holiday, a geographic name.

* ⌢   *close up.*   Join together as one word—them͡selves.

* comp   *comparison.*   Use the correct word-form, preposition, pronoun or auxiliary required in a comparison.

concl   *conclusion.*   Add a conclusion, or rewrite a weak conclusion.

con   *connection.*   Use an appropriate connection within a paragraph.

SYMBOL CHART FOR CORRECTION OF COMPOSITIONS

coor   *coordination.*   Too many short sentences have been written separately or joined by *and.* Subordinate some of the sentences.

dangl   *dangling.*   Correct the *-ing* or *-ed* phrase that has no subject to be attached to.

                 DANGLING: While *watching* TV, *her dinner* was burning on the stove.
                 CORRECTION: While watching TV, she didn't notice that her dinner was burning on the stove.
                         OR: While she was watching TV, her dinner was burning on the stove.

*frag   *fragment.*   Do not cut off a part of a sentence from the rest.

                 FRAGMENT: She has many hobbies. *For example, tennis and dancing.*
                 CORRECTION: She has many hobbies, for example, tennis and dancing.
                         OR: She has many hobbies. Among them are tennis and dancing.

*H   *hyphen.*   Correct or add a hyphen within a word or at the end of a line. Do not use a hyphen at the beginning of a line.

inform   *informal.*   Change the informal expression to one that is more appropriate for formal English.

intro   *introduction.*   Add an introduction, or rewrite a weak introduction.

*neg   *negative.*   Avoid the use of a double negative.

                 DOUBLE NEGATIVE: There isn't nobody here.
                     CORRECTION: There isn't anybody here.
                            OR: There's nobody here.

*N   *number (of nouns and adjectives).*   Use the correct singular or plural form for a noun.
Adjectives do not have any plural form except for *this* (plural *these*), *that* (plural *those*), *much* (plural *many*), *little* (plural *few*).

par   *paragraph development.*   The paragraph does not develop one main point, or it includes more than one point, or its main point is not sufficiently developed.

         ¶   *new paragraph.*   The paragraph is too long, or the wording suggests that you are turning to another aspect of the point you are developing, or a new point is being made.

         no ¶   *no new paragraph.*   This paragraph is very closely related to the one that precedes it.
Avoid single sentence paragraphs.

         //   *parallelism.*   Use the same grammatical form for word groups connected by words like *and, or, than.*

                 FAULT IN PARALLELISM: The girl promised to stay home that week and that she would study for her tests.
                         CORRECTION: The girl promised to stay home that week and to study for her tests.

SYMBOL CHART FOR CORRECTION OF COMPOSITIONS

prep *preposition.* Correct the preposition fault.

*pro *pronoun.* Correct the pronoun fault. The fault may be:
1. an incorrect form of the pronoun
2. a confusion between *it* and *there*
3. a vague or unclear reference of a pronoun
4. a change in pronoun number (singular or plural)
5. a shift in person (*we, you, one*) in a general statement
6. an unnecessary pronoun

*P *punctuation.* Correct the punctuation. Watch especially for a comma or a semicolon that has been added or omitted. Correct a run-on sentence (two sentences incorrectly joined into one by a comma or no punctuation) by using a period or a semicolon.

> RUN-ON: I will have to read more in college, consequently I will improve my reading skill.
>
> CORRECTION: I will have to read more in college; consequently I will improve my reading skill.

repet *repetitious.* Cut out the unnecessary expressions or ideas that repeat what has already been said.

*SS *sentence structure.* Supply the missing subject, verb, or object. Or correct the form of a phrase used as a subject or an object.

*sp *spelling.* Use the correct spelling. Observe the rules for doubling final consonants, keeping or dropping final *e*, changing *y* to *i*, combining the letters *i* and *e*.

*trans *transition.* Rewrite the opening sentence of a paragraph so that it connects with the preceding paragraph, or so that it makes the point of the paragraph clear.

lead-in transition. Add a connection, or rewrite a weak connection between the general statements of the introduction and the beginning of the specific topic of the composition.

vague *vague.* Make the expression or the statement more specific in relation to the point being made.

*V *verb.* Use the correct verb tense, verb form, or auxiliary.

FORM: **be +** ____-*ing* (progressive)
          be + ____-*ed* (passive)
          have + ____-*ed* (perfect tenses)

will / do / may / must / can / should + ____-(no ending)

Use the *-ing* form of a verb after a preposition.

*WF *word form.* Use the correct ending for the word (determined by the word's part-of-speech function in the sentence).

SYMBOL CHART FOR CORRECTION OF COMPOSITIONS

*WO   *word order.*   Use the correct word order for: questions and indirect questions; adverbials; adjectives.
Do not separate a verb and its object.

∽   Reverse the word order.

wordy   *wordy.*   Remove the excessive wording that has been used for the idea being expressed.

*WW   *wrong word.*   Choose the exact word for the intended meaning.

Index

a, 5-8
  with noncountable nouns, 7
Ability:
  can, be able to, 77
Absolute constructions, 48-49
  punctuation, 37-38
Abstract noun phrase, 111
  exercise, 111-13
Addition:
  transitional expression, 58
Adjective clause, 48, 117
  exercise, 117-18, 119-20, 120-21
  with parenthetic phrases, 119
Adjective phrases:
  punctuation, 37-38
Adjective structures (adjectivals), 117-122
  types, 117
    exercise, 117-18
  punctuation, 121-22
    exercise, 122
Adjectives:
  identifying characteristics, 105
  as noun modifiers, 100-101
  plural form, 25
  position, 87
  sequence, 87
  word forms, 83
Adverbial clauses:
  types, 125-28
    exercise, 128-30
Adverbial elements:
  commas, 38
Adverb structures (adverbials), 123-30
  position, 123
  punctuation, 123
  types, 123
    exercise, 123-24
Adverbs:
  identifying characteristics, 108
    exercise, 109
  as verb modifiers, 100-101
  word forms, 84
Adverbs and adverbial expressions:
  position, 85-87
Adversative clause, 127
Advisability:
  should, ought to, had better, 77
after:
  unacceptable use, 91
Agreement:
  pronoun agreement, 34
  between subject and verb, 3-4, 24-25, 73
Alternative:
  transitional expression, 58
Ambiguity:
  with adverbials, 86-87
  in comparison, 12
  with pronouns, 33
and:
  followed by a pronoun object, 33
  overcoordination, 16
  unacceptable comma, 43
and, or:
  commas in a series, 39-40
  coordination of dependent clauses and phrases, 48
  multiplication of elements in the sentence pattern, 47
  parallelism, 27-28

INDEX

another:
  unacceptable use, 36
Apostrophe, 4–5
Appositive phrases, 49
arrive:
  with *in, at,* 29–30
Article, 5–8
  in comparison, 11
  with countable, noncountable nouns, 6
Auxiliary:
  agreement with the subject, 73
  in comparison, 12
  modal, 76–78
    forms, 76
    meanings, 77–78
  with questions, negatives, 66
  types, 63

be able to:
  ability, 77
be used to:
  present custom, 78

can:
  ability, 77
  permission, 77
can–could:
  possibility, 78
Capital letter, 8–9
Cause:
  adverbial clauses, 125–26
  transitional expressions, 58
Central core of sentence and modifiers, 100–101
  exercise, 102
Clauses:
  combined, 47–48
Close up, 9–10
Coherence (*See* Connection, Transition)
Collective noun:
  agreement, 4
Colloquial words:
  informal, 21
Colon, 40
Commas:
  in combined sentences, 39
  in direct speech, 40
  with interrupting elements, 38–39
  with introductory, final elements, 37–38
  optional, 37, 37 (footnote), 39
  in a series, 39–40
  unacceptable commas, 41–43
Comparison, 10–12
  adverbial clauses, 127–28
  articles in comparison, 11

forms for comparison of adjectives, 10–11
omission and substitution in comparison, 11–12
organization for comparison, xi–xii
prepositions and conjunctions in comparison, 11
transitional expressions, 58
Complements, 94
  in sentence patterns, 95
    exercise, 96, 97–98
  two complements, 47
Complex structures, 110–30
  adjective structures (adjectivals), 117–122
  adverb structures (adverbials), 123–30
  noun structures (nominals), 110–16
Compound words:
  word division, 20
  written as one word, 10
Concessive clause, 126–27
Conclusion, 12–13
Condition:
  adverbial clause, 127
  transitional expressions, 58
  unreal conditions, 71
Conjecture, 71
Conjunctions:
  in comparison, 11
  as connectors, 101
Conjunctive adverbs:
  punctuation, 39
Connection, 13–15
Continuity, xii–xiii
  in paragraphs, 15, 26
Continuous (*See* Progressive forms of the tenses)
Contractions, 4–5
  informal, 21
  with subjects, 4–5
  with verbs, 4
Contrast:
  adverbial clauses, 126–27
  transitional expressions, 58
Coordinate conjunctions:
  unacceptable commas, 43
Coordination, 15–16

Dangling, 16–17
Dash, 41
Dependent clause, 48
Direct object, 87
  in sentence patterns, 95
    exercises, 96, 97–98
do auxiliary:
  for negatives and questions, 66
Double negative, 23
during:
  unacceptable use, 91

INDEX

each, every:
   agreement, 3
even:
   unacceptable use, 91
even though:
   unacceptable use, 91
Example:
   transitional expression, 58
Exclamations:
   exercise, 99
   word order, 88
Expectation:
   should, ought to, 77

finally, at last, 59 (footnote)
Fragment, 17-18
Future perfect tense, 69
Future tense, 68

General statements:
   pronouns, 34-35
Geographic names:
   with capital letters, 8
   with *the,* 7
Gerund phrase, 48-49, 111
   exercise, 111-13
Gerunds, 74
   after verbs, 75

had better:
   obligation, advisability, 77
have:
   auxiliary with verbals, 74
   as second auxiliary, 64
have to:
   necessity, 77
here, there:
   for connection, 14
Historical present tense, 72-73
Hyphen, 18-21
   within words, 18-19
   word division, 19-20

Imperative use of the verb, 71
Independent clause, 48
Indirect object, 87, 96-97
   exercise, 97-98
Indirect questions:
   sequence of tenses, 72
   word order, 85
Inference:
   must, 78
Infinitive phrase, 48-49, 111
   exercise, 111-13
Informal usage, 21
   in adjective clauses, 32-33, 119

Instructions:
   should, must, 78
Interjection, 101
Intransitive verb:
   in sentence patterns, 95
      exercise, 96
Introduction, 21-22
Irregular verbs, 79-82
it:
   expletive, 33
   unacceptable use, 35-36
it, they:
   used loosely, 35

Lead-in transitions, 57
   faults, 57
Linking verb:
   in sentence patterns, 95
      exercise, 96

Manner:
   adverbial clauses, 128
   transitional expressions, 59
may:
   permission, 77
may-might:
   possibility, 78
Means:
   transitional expressions, 59
Modal auxiliaries, 76-78
   forms, 76
   meanings, 77-78
most:
   agreement, 3
   followed by *of,* 8, 30
most, some, all:
   agreement, 3
must:
   inference, 78
   instructions, 78
   necessity, 77
   recommendation, 78

Necessity:
   must, have to, need to, 77
Need to:
   necessity, 77
Negative, 22-23
   requiring reversal of subject and auxiliary, 85
Negatives and questions, 66
no, 22-23
no matter:
   unacceptable use, 91
Noncountable nouns, 24-25
   agreement, 3

INDEX

Nonrestrictive structures:
    commas, 38-39
not, 22
Noun clauses, 48, 111, 113-15
    exercises, 111-13, 115-16
    punctuation, 115
    types, 113-14
    verb forms, 115
    word order, 85, 115
Nouns:
    in central core, 100
    identifying characteristics, 103
        exercise, 104
    made negative, 22-23
    number, 23-25
    word forms, 83
Noun structures (nominals), 110-16
    types, 110-11
        exercise, 111-13
Number (of nouns and adjectives), 23-25

Objective complement:
    exercise, 97-98
Objects:
    direct and indirect, 87
        exercise, 96-98
Obligation, advisability:
    should, ought to, had better, 77
of:
    after *most*, 20
-one, -body, -thing, -where, 10
One of the:
    agreement, 25
only, so:
    required reversal of subject and auxiliary, 85
Opening sentences of paragraphs, 57
    faults, 58
or, nor:
    agreement, 3
other in comparison, 12
other, the other, the others, 36
ought to:
    expectation, 77
    obligation, advisability, 77
Outline:
    in comparison, xi, xii
    parallelism, 28
Overcoordination, 15-16

Paragraphs, xiii, 25, 27
Parallelism, 27-28
    for connection, 14
Parenthetic phrases:
    in adjective clauses, 119

Participial phrases, 117
    exercise, 117-18
    punctuation, 37-38
Parts of speech, 100-109
    central core, 100
    connectors, 101
    exercise, 102
    interjections, 101
    modifiers, 100-101
Past custom:
    used to, would, 78
Past perfect tense, 68-69, 70-71
Past progressive tense, 70
Past tense, 68
Permission:
    may, can, 77
Person, 62 (footnote)
Place:
    adverbial clauses, 125
    prepositions, 29
    reversal of subject and auxiliary, 85
    transitional expressions, 59
Plurals:
    adding *-es*, 50
    nouns, 23-25
Position:
    adverb structures, 123
Possessives:
    apostrophes, 5
Possibility:
    may-might, can-could, 78
Predicate, 94
Predicate adjective:
    in sentence patterns, 95
    exercise, 96
Predicate noun:
    in sentence patterns, 95
    exercise, 96
Prefer, 31
Preference:
    would rather, 78
Prefixes:
    close up, 10
    spelling changes, 51-52
Prefixes and suffixes:
    word division, 20
Preposition, 29-32
    in comparison, 11
    as connectors, 101
    faults, 30-31
    followed by gerunds, 74
    repetition, 30
    with separable verbs, 88-89
    after verbs of speaking, 31-32
Present custom:
    be used to, 78
Present tense, 61
    for future time, 70-71
Present perfect tense, 68

INDEX

Present progressive tense, 67
Progressive forms of the tenses, 61, 65
  with *while,* 70
Pronouns, 32-36
  in comparison, 11-12
  for connections, 13-14
  faults, 33-36
  forms, 32
  as noun substitutes, 101
Proportion, xiii
Punctuation, 37-44
  marks:
    colons, 40
    commas, 37-40
      unacceptable commas, 41-43
    dashes, 41
    semicolons, 39, 40-41
      unacceptable semicolons, 43-44
  structures:
    adjective structures, 121-22
      exercise, 122
    adverb structures, 123
    noun clauses, 115
Purpose:
  adverbial clauses, 127
  transitional expressions, 59

Questions:
  exercise, 96-97
  word order, 84-85
Questions, negatives, 66
Quotation marks, 40

Recommendation:
  should, must, 78
Reinforcement:
  transitional expressions, 59
Relative pronouns, 119
  exercise, 120
Repetition:
  for connection, 14
Repetition or restatement:
  transitional expressions, 59
Repetitious, 44-45
Restrictive structures:
  punctuation, 38
Result:
  adverbial clauses, 127
  transitional expressions, 59
Reversal of subject and auxiliary:
  initial negative, 85
  after expressions of place, 85
  after *only, so,* 85
Run-on sentence, 42-43

's, s' with nouns, 5
Semicolons, 40-41
  in combined independent sentences, 39
  unacceptable semicolons, 43-44
Sentence patterns, 47-49, 95
  combinations of sentence patterns, 47-48
  expansion of sentence patterns, 47
  multiplication of elements in sentence patterns, 47
  reduction of sentence patterns, 48-49
Sentence structures:
  omission of the subject, 45
  omission of the object, 45-46
  omission of the verb, 45
  summary, 46-49
Sentences:
  parts, 94
  types, 98
Separable verbs, 88-89
Sequence (order):
  transitional expressions, 59
Sequence of tenses, 72 (*See also* Indirect questions)
shall, will, 64
should:
  expectation, 77
  instructions, 78
  obligation, advisability, 77
  recommendation, 78
Simple present tense, 67
Space (*See* Place)
Spelling, 49-56
  160 frequently misspelled words, 55-56
  rules for adding final elements, 50, 51
  rules for *ie* or *ei* words, 50
  spelling changes in prefixes before certain letters, 51-52
  word pairs often confused, 53-55
Subject, 94
Subjunctive use of the tense forms, 71-72
Subordinate clause (*See* Dependent clause)
Subordinate conjunctions:
  in adverbial clauses, 125-28
such:
  with *a,* 7
  for connection, 14
Suffixes:
  close up, 10
  spelling rules for added suffixes, 50-51
Summary, conclusion:
  transitional expressions, 59

Tenses, 61-73
  forms, 61-66
  uses, 67-73

INDEX

than:
    parallelism, 27
that:
    relative pronoun, 33
the, 5-8
    with adjectives used as nouns, 8
    with comparatives, 8
    with countable, noncountable nouns, 6
    with geographic names, 7
    in an *of* phrase, 30
    with superlatives, 7
the number of:
    agreement, 4
there:
    expletive, 33
this, that:
    for connection, 14
    pronoun faults, 34
Time:
    adverbial clauses, 125
    prepositions, 29
    transitional expressions, 59
to:
    with indirect objects, 87
Transition between paragraphs, 57-59
    lead-in transitions, 57
        faults, 57
    opening sentences of paragraphs, 57
        faults, 58
Transitional expressions, 58-59
    for connection, 14
Transitive verbs:
    in sentence patterns, 95
        exercise, 96

Uncountable nouns (*See* Noncountable nouns)
Understanding sentences, 94-99
Unity:
    in paragraphs, 25-26
Unreal conditions, 71-72
used to:
    past custom, 78

Vague, 59-60
Verbals, 73-76
    forms, 73-74
    gerunds, 74
    after verbs of physical perception, 74
Verb, 60-82
    active or passive voice, 64-65
    agreement with the subject, 73
    in central core, 100
    endings, 62
    forms, 61-66
        in noun clauses, 115
    identifying characteristics, 107
        exercise, 107
    imperative form, 71
    irregular, 79-82
    modal auxiliaries, 76-78
    negative, 22-23
    negatives and questions, 66
    perfect tenses, 65
    progressive forms of the tenses, 61, 65
    separable, 88-89
    sequence of tenses, 72
    subjunctive, 71-72
    tenses, 67-73
    verbals, 73-76
    word forms, 84

what:
    with *a*, 7
    unacceptable use, 36
where, 30
which:
    indefinite reference, 35
    relative pronoun, 32-33
while:
    with progressive forms of verbs, 70
who:
    relative pronoun, 32-33
who, which:
    in adjective clauses, 120
Wishes, 71
Word division:
    use of hyphens, 19-20
Word form (forms, markers, function, position), 83-84
    adjectives, 83
    adverbs, 84
    nouns, 83
    verbs, 84
Word order, 84-89
    for connection, 14
    in noun clauses, 115
Word pairs often confused, 53-55
Words frequently misspelled, 55-56
Wordy, 89-90
would:
    past custom, 78
would rather:
    preference, 78
Wrong word, 90
    pairs that may be confused, 90-91